I Know that Name

Paul Carrack: a Tribute

By E.J. Huntley

Designed and printed by Pickards.org.uk
Unit 1, 104 Fitzwalter Road, Sheffield S2 2SP
Telephone 0114 275 7222
www.youbooks.co.uk

Acknowledgements:

The author especially wishes to thank
Alan Wood at the Alan Wood Agency, Mark McNulty
and John Surguy for all their help
during the writing of this book.

Dedicated to: Mrs Sylvia B.

Front Cover Photograph Courtesy of Mark McNulty.

Chapter One

Paul Melvyn Carrack was born on 22nd April 1951, the youngest of two brothers (elder sibling John was born in 1947) into a large, extended working class family in Sheffield, South Yorkshire.

Paul would spend his formative years in Crookes, about a mile and a half outside of Sheffield's city centre, where his Mum and Dad ran a shop that sold wallpaper and paint. Paul's dad worked as a self-employed painter and decorator while Mum ran the shop, at the back of which the Carracks lived.

Back then Crookes was still relatively semi-rural. Overlooking the Rivelin Valley and boasting the picturesque Bole Hill park, Crookes would be an idyllic place to grow up.

"I grew up in the outskirts of Sheffield, [which was] much more of a village atmosphere," Carrack later reminisced, "[We had] a lot of freedom as kids and we played out on the streets all the time. We were told there may be danger out there but we weren't really conscious of that ... and it was a great time, a lot less complicated, I think, than these days."

Although Sheffield, like the rest of post war Britain, was pretty austere back then, Carrack's parents were dedicated to making life better for their young family and were determined to instil in their two boys the values of "hard work, honesty and treating people with respect" that would stand them in good stead for the rest of their lives.

Although football and Sheffield Wednesday were his first loves Carrack was bitten by the musical bug from an early age: "My father particularly was the musical influence and his family had some musical connections and my aunts played piano, my Grandmother played piano and in the attic above the shop where we lived I found some bits of old drum kit and that's kind of how I got started, playing along would you believe, to a wind up gramophone and bashing these bits of old drum kits."

Presumably to the annoyance of his neighbours, Carrack would practice constantly, commandeering his parents attic and teaching himself to play by bashing along to records on an old wind-up gramophone! Fortunately Paul's father was a constant source of encouragement, sticking wallpaper around the old fashioned kit, "to make it look nice."

Carrack also received encouragement at school and years later he would recall a teacher who was a particular inspiration: "I remember when I was a little kid I used to stand next to Mr. Holden, one of the teachers. I could never understand what was going on. This guy was a music teacher and he used to sing counterpoint to all the hymns. And I thought, "What's going on here?," 'cause he's singing the wrong tune yet it's all working. I used to always try to get near this guy ... he was an incredible guy. He wrote this whole opera for little kids, based on the Barber of Seville. He played fiddle, and come to think of it, I starred in one of his shows."

Paul's happy childhood, though, was shattered at the tender age of eleven when his father died unexpectedly after an accident at work: "I came home from school one day and they weren't here because unfortunately my dad had had an accident. A ladder had come down on him and he trapped his neck in between the ladder rungs and broke his neck and three days later he passed away."

"In that time they didn't really know how to treat spinal injuries so they drilled two holes in his head and used weights to try and pull his spine back into position but it didn't happen."

For Paul the news was understandably earth-shattering and he would admit that he carried a strong sense of loss around for many years: "I'd had such a happy upbringing that for Dad to die just seemed unfathomable."

"It was a massive blow because I did love him to bits. He was a fantastic guy and it's a real massive shock and it takes a long time to get over and I don't think you probably ever do; it does stay with you... It was a big shock and a big heartbreak and I think in a way it kind of influenced me musically ... because I tend to lean to that melancholy thing and I have a well of stuff that I can draw on."

Paul's brother John, then aged just fifteen, effectively took over as the head of the household as well as the running of the shop and became (and remains) a strong guiding influence in Paul's life.

"After my father died, school was a nightmare," Paul admits. "Nothing could make me get out of bed in the mornings and I remember my brother John having to force me to get up. I ended up being quite rebellious."

One of Paul's coping strategies was to throw himself deeper into his music.

"I think music became my way of getting over his death," he acknowledged. "The first Christmas after it happened my mum bought me a drum kit on hire purchase, as a way of cheering me up, I suppose. It was the bee's knees."

Another timely arrival in Carrack's life was the Mersey Beat boom - and it was this that really ignited Carrack's desire to pursue a career in music.

"I was always interested in music wherever I could get it. You know it wasn't so much around in those days; on the radio if you heard a pop record on it was quite something. [My brother] played guitar and he would bring home all kinds of records - blues records and soul records and of course when the Beatles happened [Paul would see the Fab Four play at the Sheffield City Hall on three occasions] and the whole Mersey Beat thing I got bitten very badly by the musical bug and that was it and there was no looking back really."

Paul soon formed his first band - the Saville Row Rhythm Unit - with his cousin Robert Batty on bass and a friend Johnny Whitham on guitar both of whom, like Paul were aged around fourteen / fifteen.

Paul would later claim that one of the main reasons he had formed a band was because it was the only way he could get into some of the city's clubs to the see the bands he idolised: "They wouldn't let me in because I was small and young. At the Mojo they would vet you outside and I got turned away in front of some of the girls in my class which was a super embarrassment, so I got into a band so I could get in. I did get into the Mojo once when the Hollies were on, it was something like ten bob to get in, so I paid and got in and they were absolutely brilliant."

Even many years later Paul could still remember Saville Row's earliest gigs: "I remember playing the woodwork teacher's wedding and they had a whip round and we got twenty-eight shillings I think for that but probably before that we played at the school concert. We did four Beatles songs and the kids in the audience all played their part by screaming and throwing jelly babies at us."

Despite their inexperience and youth in January 1966 Saville Row entered a Battle of the Bands contest at the Esquire club organised by Unit 19, Sheffield's first independent recording studio.

Incredibly they beat off stiff competition from the rest of the field to scoop first prize, although as Paul would later concede their victory probably wasn't a fair reflection of his band's actual ability: "It was a fiddle how that happened. We took all our mates along and it was based on audience response. There was this older band on who were a proper good band and they were a bit miffed when we won it."

Saville Row's prize for winning the competition was a day inside Unit 19 and it would prove to be a life changing day for the young drummer, it being his first encounter with the instrument with which he would become most closely associated - the Hammond Organ.

"We got our day in the recording studio," Paul reminisced, "and inside the recording studio was a Hammond Organ and bear in mind I'm a drummer at this point. I turned the Hammond Organ on and the engineer showed me a few chords and that was the first time I'd seen how to play chords on a keyboard."

Shortly after this Saville Row were joined by singer Clive Morris, and were soon showing a marked improvement. The band's progress, though, was halted when Morris was poached by local soul band, The Reaction, much to Carrack's chagrin.

"I was dead jealous," Paul recalled. "I went to see Reaction at the Silver Blades and I thought they were fantastic."

Fortunately Clive promised to get Paul in The Reaction but only if he ditched the drums and bought an organ. Paul duly obliged.

Just as he had with the drums, Paul eschewed lessons and opted instead to teach himself how to play: "I'm sure that there were about fifty-thousand groups across England called the Reaction at that time, but this particular Reaction was a seven or eight piece, with a brass section. I used to put Jimmy Smith records on at 16rpm and try to cop a few licks. That's how I learned to play; I haven't had any training whatsoever. When I was starting out, providing we were in the key of C, I could do a pretty fair impersonation of Jimmy Smith. Anything else, and I was lost."

Although progress at first was slow, Carrack developed quickly, as Morris recalls: "We used to practice down at my dad's big house on Burngreave Road and some of the band went up the wall about his playing. But I said, "Well if he goes, I go." And he learned quickly how to play, just sailed. In about a month he was good at holding chords and he was starting to get rhythms going."

"He really surprised me when he started playing," drummer Brian Watson remembers, "he used to have a little Selmer Capri organ, we used to call it 'Plastic 'Un.' It sounded like Sooty!"

Joining the Reaction would see Carrack moving away from his early Mersey Beat influences into a more soulful terrain.

"Soul was the music of the times," Carrack reminisced, "and the king of the scene was Geno Washington and the Ram Jam Band whose Hand Clappin', Foot Stompin', Funky-Butt ... Live album we played more or less verbatim. This was the most influential period for me musically."

"Although I wasn't singing at this point, I loved all the greats," Paul enthused, "particularly David Ruffin, Stevie Wonder, Marvin Gaye, Smokey Robinson and hundreds of others."

By the time it came for Paul to take his GCEs it was clear that music had completely taken priority over his education.

"I was absolutely hopeless at school," Paul admits. "I've never been very academically minded. I left school at sixteen; in fact the van was waiting at school when I was taking my GCEs. I took an exam in the morning [and] I had one in the afternoon. I came out at lunchtime and the boys said, "no, we're going to Scotland, we've got to go now." So that was it."

Although Carrack did briefly work for the gas board when he left school he was determined to pursue a career in music, a notion that he concedes was not "considered a very respectable carry on at all," particularly by his mum.

"My mum was very wary of the whole idea of trying to make your living as a musician," Carrack explains, "well, she was probably quite right especially back then it it was a very flaky way of making a crust."

"Work was pretty sacred where I grew up and having a job was the be-all and end-all. My folks had a very tough existence themselves growing up through the 1920s and 1930s and then there was the war, so they were desperate for a bit of security."

"There was a lot of employment around in those days and most people went for the security of a job in the many industries and spin off industries in Sheffield and I guess playing in a band was considered playing pretty low life."

"We had the shop but I didn't fit into that and I just knew what I wanted to do. I wanted to be one of those guys who went off in a van down the road."

Although life on the road appeared glamorous, it wasn't all fun and games and Clive Morris would recall how Paul's youth and boyishness made him a target for some unwanted attention: "[Our manager / driver] fancied Paul something wicked. I remember once we played this club and the manager brought this guy to see us and he liked the band but he liked Paul more. Paul wasn't having any of that at all and I think we lost the contract."

In October 1967 the Reaction split up following a petty row. "It was purely over petrol money - a few pence," guitarist Glyn Owen revealed. "The manager wanted some money for petrol. He said, "I must have some money off somebody," and four stayed in and three got out. It was as simple as that."

"Clive argued and did this big bluff and we ended up getting out and walking home from Leeds," Paul recollects. "It was pitch black so there was no chance of getting a lift and we got as far as Chapeltown before we got a lift as it got daylight."

Since there were still some outstanding gigs to complete Carrack, Watson, Owen and Dick Crews on bass soldiered on. With Clive no longer in the picture Paul took over the lead vocal duties.

"That's when Paul got to grips with a lot of the singing," Owen reflects, "and he made it quite clear that he'd got a good soulful voice. He certainly showed his colours by doing all the introductions and doing a show as it should've been and he played great Hammond organ by then."

Despite the great strides he was making as a musician, it was clear that the circuit he was playing was becoming something of a treadmill. In addition, musical fashions were starting to move away from the soul music Carrack and his bandmates were playing.

"We were at rock bottom," Glyn Owen admits, "the soul thing was giving way to early Clapton and a bit of psychedelia. All the gear was falling apart and we had to resort to doing our first working men's club, the Tramways at York ... We had no plug-board and Dick Crews got electrocuted in the process of trying to wire all these mains into the wall during bingo. He got the full belt of these two wires and the irony of it was that at this great outburst of pain, all the club could say was, "Has somebody shouted house?""

Inevitably Paul realised that if he really wanted to make a career out of music he needed to get off the treadmill of gigs in and around Sheffield, and so, along with Brian Watson, Paul formed a new band called Cake with two guys they'd talent-spotted whilst gigging with The Reaction.

"We'd seen these two guys in a band called Granny's Attic from Burnley," Brian Watson explains. "They were singer Les Walker and bass player Terry 'Tex'

Comer. We went up and just said, "We want to form a band," so we formed Cake. We hardly did any gigs, just universities, but we got big money."

In an effort to get more work the band headed down to London for an audition at the Golden Star club. At stake was a month-long residency at the Storyville club in Frankfurt, Germany.

"We came down to London to do an audition at a reggae club off the Caledonian Road," Paul later recalled. "We drove through the night we kipped in the van to be there early. There was hundreds of bands there auditioning to go and play in Germany - we went for it big style did our set and they loved us. I was seventeen, the other lads were probably have been eighteen / nineteen and we went off to Frankfurt."

It seems though that there was a catch attached to the gig in Frankfurt, when the band were persuaded to take on two additional members. "We passed an audition and they came up with these two girl singers, two sisters," Brian Watson remembers. "They were like Janis Joplin and they couldn't half sing."

It seems there was also a plan afoot to turn the newly formed co-ed sextet into chart toppers courtesy of the pen of Tony MacAuley - who had co-written Baby Now That I've Found You and Build Me Up Buttercup for The Foundations, Love Grows (Where My Rosemary Goes) for Edison Lighthouse and would later write Don't Give Up on Us for David Soul.

"There was this guy called Tony MacAuley who wrote songs for all these daft acts like the Paper Dolls," Watson continues. "And they wanted us to be the next Paper Dolls with these two chicks but we weren't having any of that."

Nevertheless the girls, Rita and Tina, remained which evidently necessitated a name change, Cake becoming The Milwaukee Coasters.

A residency in the clubs of Germany was almost a rite of passage for any aspiring musician in the 1960s, a path most famously pioneered by The Beatles and the rest of their Mersey Beat comrades.

As it had been for The Beatles and the rest Frankfurt, Cologne and Hamburg would be Carrack's musical apprenticeship, but while the brutal working hours he and his colleagues were forced to play would improve their musicianship they truly were all-night tests of endurance.

"We played for hours and hours a night," Carrack confirms, "and this was our grounding and how we got to learn our trade really. It was very hand to mouth I've got to say. But for us it was an adventure."

"We didn't really think in terms of having a break," Paul adds. "It was just playing and playing gigs and meeting girls and having fun [and] that was as far as our ambitions went; we didn't even dream of making records and stuff until later."

As it transpired that chapter of his career was just around the corner.

Chapter Two

Although his regular trips to Germany were exciting times for Paul, allowing him as they did the chance to hone his chops, see a little bit of the world and no doubt some eye-opening life experiences (the late George Harrison called Hamburg, "the naughtiest city in the world"), he and his colleagues were quickly outgrowing the nightly diet of covers they were expected to play.

Whilst on the look out for a new direction fate intervened during one stint at Hamburg's Top Ten Club when the Coasters met up with a band from Southport called Jasmin-T (who had recorded the music for and briefly appeared in British cult slasher film The Haunted House starring Frankie Avalon and Dennis Price - filmed in their hometown), who included in their ranks the multi-instrumentalists John Surguy and Alan Solomon.

The guys in the Coasters (who now included Dave Pepper who had replaced the departed Brian Watson) were blown away by the duo (who were also disillusioned with their band's direction) and invited them to jam.

As John Surguy recalls the two groups of musicians hit it off immediately: "Because the times we played were very long, five forty-five minute sets per night, one hour on, one hour off, the two bands would start to jam together, sometime one song would last forty-five minutes, the manager of the club [a man named Ricky Barnes, formerly one of the tenor sax players with Lord Rockingham's X1, who had had a big hit with Hoots Mon] thought this was great because being a sax player himself he loved the sound of the baritone and tenor together. The two bands played there together for one month, and I think we started to realise then, that we had the makings of a new band."

Although everyone went their separate ways at the end of this particular residency, the guys stayed in touch when they returned to England and when Jasmin-T split up shortly afterwards Surguy and Solomon contacted Les and Paul to see if they wanted to form a new group. The two girl singers were ditched and, in June 1969, Warm Dust was born.

The new sextet assembled in Burnley and spent the next few months rehearsing and writing new songs that bore little relation to the covers that had formed their Hamburg sets. Sensing that rock and roll was moving in a more progressive direction and having recently discovered mind enhancing drugs and the equally enlightening literature of the underground press, Warm Dust decided to follow suit.

"Basically, we discovered pot and we decided we were going to go progressive," Paul Carrack recalls. "In Hamburg we met these two guys ... John Surguy and Alan Solomon. They played saxes, flutes, oboes, the lot... We were listening to the Mothers of Invention, Hot Rats, Freak Out, the Beatles' White Album and Jimmy Smith at half-speed to analyse it."

"The band was very influenced by Frank Zappa and we use to listen to all his albums," Surguy agreed. "Les used to write all of the words but the rest of the band would add their own musical style which is why some of the songs we did could last for twenty minutes or more. I'm not sure what the word progressive music really meant, but to me, it just seemed to be a progression from the three-minute songs of the 1960s to the longer over twenty-minute songs of the 1970s, where bands were experimenting with different tempos, key signatures, etc. all in the same song, like Genesis and Yes."

Armed with their new sound Warm Dust returned to the Top Ten Club and, after playing there for a month, the band set out on their first of many tours of Europe with a band from South Wales called Man who had evolved from the remnants of chart group The Bystanders.

"Man was the only other British group we liked," Carrack later extolled. "We played with them at the Paradiso in Amsterdam and they did all this avant-garde free-form stuff. Bing Bong! The [audience] thought it was fantastic."

When they returned to the UK the band would initially always head back to Lancashire.

"We all use to live in Burnley," Surguy told me. "Les and Terry lived there, and the rest of us would stay with their parents or friends, even the road crew lived there."

Eventually the band moved down to London where they lived in a variety of squats. Although the band's lifestyle was very hand to mouth at this stage, Carrack et al didn't seem to mind; music was still the be all and end all.

"At the time, our music was our whole life," Paul Carrack confirms. "We were relatively unambitious. We only wanted to be as big as Family or The Nice because they had the big P.A.s and the Marshall rigs, and a few roadies. That was the ambition. It was very uncool to be ambitious back then, but you had to have the accoutrements. We would have liked the house in the country. It would have been like the Young Ones, except we were all Neil."

Although Warm Dust spent most of the first few months of 1970 touring mainland Europe in their van (which they christened "the mothership") the group did secure some notable bookings back home - playing in March, for example, a well-publicised date at the Lyceum Ballroom in London with the Salvation Army Choir backing the band on a sprawling suite entitled And it Came to Pass.

Apparently Keith Moon also joined the band on stage at this gig - "drunk as a skunk, jamming on congas" according to Les Walker's memories. John Surguy, though, claims not to remember The Who's drummer even being there. Perhaps if you do remember, you weren't really there!

Having shopped around the band's demos, the band's manager, Del Taylor (who would later manage Alexis Korner and Jim Diamond), somehow secured a deal with an obscure jazz label, Trend Records.

"I'm not really sure how the deal with Trend Records came about," Surguy recalls, "all I know is, at that time, there were lots of small record labels starting up and Del Taylor got us the deal, I'm not even sure what the deal was, we were just concentrating on the music, and it was important that we had something to show to our fans."

Bravely, the band's debut album - And It Came to Pass (produced by John Worsely) - would be a double, dominated by lengthy suites with extended instrumental passages, portentous and thought-provoking lyrics, dense arrangements, challenging time signatures, complicated instrumental interplay and the occasional free-form wig out.

The eleven-minute Turbulance (sic), with its hippy-ish "Get yourself together, know where you're going" refrain, is very much of its time lyrically but the music provides the perfect introduction to Warm Dust. All the ingredients that defined the band are present and correct.

In Les Walker (who, for this album, had re-christened himself as the more exotic Dransfield Walker) the band possessed an exceptionally fine singer with a strong rock-blues voice, a highly accomplished bass player in Tex Comer, and although Carrack's dexterous nimble-fingered Hammond playing is given plenty of room to shine it is the fluid and inventive jazz flute and sax interplay between Surguy and Solomon that provide the pyrotechnics in the absence of guitar.

"I'm not sure why we had no guitarist," Surguy muses. "I can only think it's because, when we started playing together, we didn't have one, and never thought of adding one, the sound we had at the time was what we wanted.

"Between myself and Alan Solomon, we covered all the sax and flute section. I played, tenor and alto sax, flute, oboe and guitar and Alan played baritone and soprano sax, flute, clarinet and keyboards, in fact he made his own synthesiser. Most of the time we would start a song where we both played flute in harmony, then move up to clarinet and oboe, then soprano and alto, then tenor and baritone, then sometime, synth and alto sax (through a Maestro effect unit, it made one sax sound like four). So we were building the song all the time."

If Turbulance was dominated in the main by soothing flutes and organ, Achromasia employs a brassier, jazzier attack, abetted by some manic Hammond stabbing from Carrack. While its adventurousness might not be to everyone's taste the song is worth the effort for the sheer audacity of the multiple key changes the riff undergoes towards the end of the song shortly before settling into a funereal New Orleans march over which Walker vocalises superbly and, at one point, unleashes a 'Rawk God' scream of which Roger Daltrey would have been proud.

After the unabashed prog of Turbulance and Achromasia, Circus and Keep on Truckin' are much more straightforward pieces. Circus is one of the more structured songs on the album with some beautiful and tight harmony passages while the band display their versatility on the kitschy twelve-bar boogie Keep on Truckin' which boasts a brilliantly deranged Hammond solo by Carrack (who also adds some fine honky tonk piano), a superbly greasy sax solo and some authentic harmonica blowing from Walker.

The album's centre-piece, though, was the ten-minute title track which depicts the before and aftermath of an atomic bomb falling on an unnamed city.

A highly eclectic tour de force And it Came to Pass shifts gears and time signature (often in mid-bar) and runs a gamut from trad jazz, Lalo Schifrin soundtrack funk, Tommy Steele novelty song, modern jazz, Stax horn riffs, a soothing pastoral organ interlude, nightmarish Sun Ra wig out, Hammer horror movie transcript and ending on an extract from the John Bunyan psalm He Who Would Valiant Be.

After the ambitious and at times disturbing title track Loosing Touch provides comparative relief. Opening with about a minute of soothing laid back flute the song explodes into an organ-driven R&B juggernaut, a style that is perfectly suited to Walker's powerful voice.

After the album's second blues, the sax-driven Blues For Pete, Man Without A Straw is another more easily digestible track, albeit with a strong psychedelic influence, sounding in places not unlike something Pink Floyd might have recorded on their second album, Saucerful of Secrets. For once Surguy's and Solomon's reeds take a back seat and allow Carrack a chance to impress with a highly inventive organ solo that the likes of Brian Auger or Richard Wright would have been pleased with.

The fourteen-minute long Wash My Eyes continues the psychedelic tone and given that this and Man Without Straw seemed perfect songs to get stoned to (although I am emphatically not speaking from experience), it seems odd that the band were not more widely embraced given prog's foothold within the mainstream around this time.

For many, though, the highlight of the album would be its closing track - a funky cover of Richie Havens' Indian Rope Man. With Carrack's best Jimmy Smith impression and Walker's powerful vocal and some especially fine playing from the entire band it's not hard to see why the track was one of their most popular pieces.

"It was the whole band's decision to record Indian Rope Man," John Surguy says, "in fact, Richie Havens was another artist we used to listen to a lot."

Remarkably the entire album was recorded in just one session! "We recorded all the backing in one take," Surguy confirms, "then recorded the vocals, all on the same day, and fell asleep on the tube on the way home, it was a good job it was only going to Cockfosters (we lived there for a few months) otherwise I'm not sure where we'd have ended up?"

Upon its release in May And it Came to Pass received mixed reviews. Although Disc magazine praised the album ("their music is full, melodic, different and with much promise for the future"), elsewhere it was dismissed as pretentious - which reportedly greatly upset the band.

"We're progressing at our own speed," Carrack protested to Disc. "That album was our first steps. The sad thing is that your offering has to be compared to other things, it seems, in order to be judged. So you compare it to something like Zappa's Hot Rats and it was average, but it was good for us."

All things considered And It Came To Pass (released in May 1970) is actually a pretty good debut effort. In fact when you consider the time constraints under which it was recorded, the amount of musical ideas the band manages to cram in is quite astonishing. It was also clear that in Carrack (belying his teenage years), Surguy and Solomon Warm Dust possessed some exceptionally gifted and original musicians who could take songs in surprising directions and could solo as well as any prog axeman, giving the band a highly distinctive and unique sound.

While And it Came to Pass failed to dent the charts in the UK, the album would prove to be enormously successful on mainland Europe - debatably prog's heartland - where, perhaps understandably, the band seemed to prefer performing.

"English audiences are a drag," Carrack complained to Disc Magazine in June 1970. "The audiences have this superior attitude. They think they've seen everything."

As a mark of how high their profile was in Germany, for example, in December the band were invited to appear on the extremely prestigious Beat Club show.

Broadcast monthly by the regional TV network Radio Bremen, Beat-Club was the first music programme in German television history (the show ran from September 1965 to December 1972). With its highly distinctive style (when colour television became popular, Beat-Club was one of the first TV shows to experiment with visual, sometimes psychedelic effects) the show would play host to virtually every touring international artist worth his or her salt during this rich period of rock and roll history. It says much, then, for Warm Dust's popularity in Germany that they were even invited to appear, given their comparative obscurity in the UK.

Screened on New Year's Eve 1970 the band (appearing alongside UFO, The Move featuring Jeff Lynne and Emerson, Lake & Palmer) performed Indian Rope Man and two versions of non-album cut - the Beatles-ish (Pepper-period) Worm Dance.

1971 would prove to be another busy year for the band commencing with the release in January of their second LP, Peace in Our Time (again produced by John Worsely), this one a concept album based on the theme of world peace, the madness of war and the band's contempt for the malevolence of the political establishment.

It was, though, as John Surguy was keen to stress, a concept that had been foisted upon them by the band's management: "Because of [And it Came to Pass], the management got the idea that we would make a complete LP about the madness of war. We did not want to do it, all we wanted to do was play music not be some kind of politicians, but they had an idea they could make a lot of money!!"

Atop the album was the group's solemn manifesto: "The history of the white, menopausal, mendacious men now ruling the Planet Earth is a history of the repeated violation of the harmonious laws of nature, all having the direct object of establishing a tyranny of the materialistic ageing over the gentle, the peace-loving, the young, the coloured. To prove this, let facts be submitted to the judgement of generations to come."

Continuing the portentous theme each of the songs on Peace in Our Time would be preceded by a monologue (delivered by Carrack in his broadest Sheffield accent) about the history of human conflict from the Second World War to the time of the album's release, from Neville Chamberlain's Peace in our Time speech, the attack on Pearl Harbour and the USA's bombing of Hiroshima and Nagasaki, the Cold War, the Korean War, Russia's invasion of Czechoslovakia, the Nigerian Civil War, to the hostilities between Israel and Palestine and in Vietnam.

Although this was heavy stuff, the band would confess to a fear of being continually labelled pretentious.

"That theme [on And it Came to Pass] wasn't strong enough to take up the whole album at the time we wrote it, but we're continuing it much further on the next album," Carrack would forewarn. "The reason we're afraid of being called pretentious is that it might do the whole peace thing damage. With Lennon doing such good things we don't want to cheapen the whole thing."

Being restricted this time to a single album format ensured the band would be more economic and focused on their sophomore effort and largely less prone to wig out than they had been on their debut. This change of direction had been a conscious decision by the band.

"During our first year we were into a musical trip, a very technical thing," Alan Solomon would later articulate to Beat Instrumental magazine. "We were trying to cram as much music as possible into every set. It was all a bit too intellectual. We suddenly realised, sometime last year, that audiences didn't want long freaky, instrumental parts. So we changed our approach.

Now we're more into rock; we're much more into writing songs. A lot of our stuff is much shorter than it used to be."

The album proper kicks off with the dramatic Blood Of My Fathers - a swampy belter driven by a hypnotic bass groove (that suggests the band had been keeping abreast of the new, harder sounds that were coming out of the funk / soul movement) and some fiesty brass accompaniment. Walker's vocals are fed through a Leslie speaker, to create an appropriately disembodied effect.

Winds of Change is a piece not unlike a couple of my own personal favourite pieces of music, Frank Zappa's Peaches en Regalia or Latona by Big John Patton. Played in a driving 6/8 time the band rock on this track, so loudly in fact that they rather bury Les Walker's vocals as a result.

Justify Things Your Hands Have Done (the longest song on the album, clocking in at almost nine minutes) meanwhile sounds like a Santana backing track shorn of its guitar. With the band perhaps realising its groove wasn't going anywhere particularly interesting the song then breaks down and strays into a bizarre interlude dominated by saxophones and Alan Solomon's new homemade synthesiser.

"I wanted something to make some of the sounds that I heard Stockhausen making," Solomon told Beat Instrumental. "I started by experimenting with sine and square-wave oscillators - although I couldn't use them on stage, because they didn't fit the music that was going then. I decided I wanted a synthesiser - so I started to make one."

After a mercifully brief drum solo the track then becomes an exercise in schmaltzy Age of Aquarius muzak, although some vague elements of discordance give it a slightly queasy and unsettling undercurrent.

Interestingly the introduction of these electronic elements by Solomon would lead to the band doing a tour of Germany with an early incarnation of Kraftwerk, a tour which proved to be very popular.

The ambient, slow-burning Rejection is one of the most chilled out songs of Warm Dust's entire canon and proves a highlight. After a brief burst of descending classical guitar (played by Surguy) the piece evolves into a bluesy Rhodes and Hammond organ driven shuffle, peppered with some lovely flute playing before evolving again into a jazzier piece (with Solomon's synthesiser again making an appearance) before ending on a brief snatch of East European folk music to which a Cossack might have enjoyed strutting his stuff.

Very Small Child, meanwhile, finds the band almost in singer-songwriter territory (the song was written by David Kubinec of Mainhorse Airplane). There are elements here that recall such sixties epics as Nights in White Satin and A Whiter Shade of Pale and a tidier, more focused production job on this could have been the sort of thing that launched Warm Dust into a bigger league.

The band then change tack on Song For A Star, a dirty, straight ahead rocker which includes a first for the band in the shape of a gnarly guitar solo. Special mention here must go to Tex Comer for his fuzz bass playing throughout which sounds like it's being fed through a cement mixer.

After the comparatively brief gospelly blues of Wrote a Letter the narration concludes with the band's audacious manifesto - the creation of a new world order and a constitution for peace: "We, the free men and free women of the planet Terra, in order to form a more perfect union re-establish species harmony, provide for the physical and spiritual sustenance, promote the general welfare of all living forms, ensure a climate of ecstatic prayer and secure the blessings of liberty to all creatures now living and their posterity, do ordain and establish this constitution for the United Tribes of Earth."

The music that follows this idealistic pipe dream, Peace of Mind, is almost a Paul Carrack solo showcase. After a brief vocal from Walker and a short-ish flute interlude Carrack's organ takes the song and the album through to its optimistic almost elegiac conclusion.

Although the well-meaning spoken word segments sound very dated now (and more than a little didactic) the music itself was a far more accomplished and coherent effort than And it Came to Pass and is something of a flawed masterpiece well overdue critical rediscovery.

Clearly the band's management and label seemed to think they had something special on their hands, spending a fortune on the album's lavish gate-fold sleeve (which included some extremely unflinching images from the conflicts name-checked) and on pressing some editions of the record on white vinyl.

To accompany the album the band released as a single the celebratory It's a Beautiful Day (backed with Worm Dance), which was a much more commercially-minded effort. Clearly written with the charts in mind the song was tipped for big things by the trade papers but sadly, like all their other UK releases, it too failed to chart.

The reason for the failure of the single - easily the most accessible thing the band had done up to this point - was partially explained by the fact that due to the record's thirty-second flute intro most radio stations had refused to play it. The song was remixed and reissued in a revised form in April but once again it failed to trouble the UK top fifty.

To promote Peace in Our Time the band's management came up with some novel and inventive new media strategies, as John Surguy recalls: "They wanted to turn us into some kind of peace envoys, so we had our own poppy day at the War Museum (with white poppies) which was screened on TV, and then chartered a small plane (with a white Dove on the side) to fly us to Rome."

Incredibly the purpose of the trip to Rome was to visit Pope Paul VI! Reportedly the band had written to the Pope and other religious and political leaders asking how they could help world peace through their music. Their letter was answered by one of the Pope's cardinals who duly arranged a meeting on 16th April 1971 (following which the group would appear at a World Peace festival, screened on Italian TV). As a result Warm Dust became the first pop group to be given a private audience with a serving Pontiff.

The band, however, were not wholly in favour of this publicity stunt. "Even though we wrote all the songs," John Surguy reveals, "we really did not want anything to do with this hype! After all, we were just musicians!"

Perhaps this explains why it was new drummer John Bedson who would be pushed forward to act as the band's mouthpiece: "I went to a Roman Catholic school but none of us think on those lines," Bedson told the Daily Sketch. "We're not religious in the orthodox way. We don't go to church every Sunday. We think that the church today is apathetic, Mind you, we'll only tell the Pope that if he asks us. We'll play it by ear."

When the big day arrived the band would meet with the Pope at the Vatican's Clementina Hall, alongside around fifty other youths from Britain, France, Canada and Italy.

After presenting His Holiness with a copy of Peace in Our Time, drummer John Bedson would issue the band's demands.

"John Bedson told the Pope that if he could ban woman Catholics from using contraceptives," Les Walker (who had sported, for the occasion, a black Superman pullover with a big red letter 'S' on the front), told the press, "he should also ban them from fighting and end conscription in Italy."

Reportedly the Pope replied that he would remember the suggestion, adding that while he and his cardinals were "not in a position to appreciate your artistic forms, nor to evaluate the aesthetic forms in which you express your personalities," he could and did "appreciate the sincerity of youth."

Despite the tremendous boost their profile had received from meeting the Pope, the band were soon distancing themselves from the peace movement.

"Somehow a lot of people saw us to be crusaders for peace," Les Walker told The Daily Sketch, "but we didn't see ourselves as a peace group at all. What we did on the album was to just make a statement and leave it at that; that is up to each individual. We just hoped that maybe people would think and make up their own minds. The only harm that the reaction led to was that we began to get a little hung up about it ourselves. We just made a statement and it was misunderstood."

Returning to the UK the band seemed to pick up a bit of momentum when they appeared on the main stage at the Reading Festival on 25th June 1971, but, despite such high-profile performances, the band couldn't seem to make the breakthrough in their home market. They did, however, continue to make further strides in mainland Europe, particularly in Scandinavia where they were now spending a great deal of their time touring.

When they returned to the UK Warm Dust embarked on a tour of colleges and polytechnics with Brian Auger's Oblivion Express during November and December, by which time the band had set up base in Potters Bar.

"This house was great," Surguy recalls, "it was out in the country, and had a garage, where we could have rehearsals."

The fruits of these rehearsals would form the basis of the band's third and final album, produced by Derek Lawrence and recorded for the German label BASF. The eponymously-titled Warm Dust would mark another change of direction.

According to Paul Carrack the band had been listening to Van Morrison's Moondance album around this time and this influence comes across strongly on the album's superb radio-friendly opener, Lead Me to the Light.

It's not hard to imagine say, The Band (or Van the Man, for that matter) writing and recording something like this to great critical acclaim. Although Walker is on fine form vocally, Carrack's influence is all over this track, from the tasteful piano accompaniment to the delightful Hammond solo and backing vocals. It sounds like a template for the sort of song he would later write for his next band, Ace.

Who knows, had this been the direction the band had taken from the outset greater commercial success might have come their way.

Although Warm Dust had tackled the blues before, Long Road marked another new direction for the band. For a starters the track is dominated by overdriven electric guitar (played by guest musician John Knightsbridge). Sounding more like The Faces, the track bore little of the style the band had essayed on their first two albums.

Similarly commercial was the funky Mister Media (released as a French single backed with And It Came to Pass's Keep on Trucking). With Comer's elastic bass lines, its conga drums, Surguy and Solomon's taut Stax horn riffs, Carrack's grooving organ and Walker's best impression of a black soul artist this was a long way from their prog image and could and perhaps should have been the song that catapulted the band into the mainstream. Although that wasn't to be it's still something of a mystery that this song isn't more widely known.

Rounding off side one was a rather pretty eight-and-a-half-minute-long cover of Richie Havens' Hole in the Future. Halfway through the band deviate into a four-and-a-half-minute interlude which can only be described as a vaguely nightmarish trip through a Moroccan souk before returning to the song they had initially set out to cover.

If much of the first side of the album suggested Warm Dust were in the process of moving away from prog (the North African detour notwithstanding), the band return to more familiar territory with the eighteen-minute long Blind Boy, that encompasses side two of the album.

Preceded by a minute-long snatch of Mussorgsky's tone poem A Night on the Bare Mountain (the Russian composer helping himself to a rare writing credit on a rock album) Blind Boy is a five-part suite that ambitiously covers so much terrain it would be take an entire chapter to cover it here. Much better, then, to recommend tracking down a copy of the album and listen to what, in the best traditions of saving the best till last, was probably Warm Dust's crowning achievement as a group.

Although the third album - which remains an unearthed gem - would once again fail to chart in the UK, it would prove to be particularly popular in Germany, climbing to #10 on their album charts.

This success later prompted the German-only release of the twelve-track compilation album, Dreams of Impossibilities, which included every track (except Blues for Pete) from the first album and three tracks from the second - Peace Of Mind, Song For A Star and Blood Of My Fathers.

Following the band's third album, drummer John Bedson left to be replaced by Steve Witherington and plans were soon afoot to record a fourth album. Although the band did cut some tracks in a German recording studio - among them I'm Sorry and Time Ain't Long (which Carrack would re-record with Ace) - all plans for a fourth LP were shelved when the band's management abruptly decided to pull the plug.

Although they had been handed their notice, there was still one last ill-fated tour to Scandinavia left in the book. On the way to Newcastle to catch the boat for Norway, 'the mothership' finally broke down. Although the band went ahead with hired equipment and a hired van, these unforeseen overheads meant the band made nothing from the tour, which proved to be the final straw.

"When we arrived back in Newcastle [in October 1972], we all just split up and went our own different ways," Surguy remembers ruefully, "I remember going to the bus station to get a bus to Burnley, but had just missed the last one, and, as I only had enough money for the bus, I had to hock my sax for the train fare (which I did get back) so after all this I was completely pissed off with the music scene (which must have lasted a couple of days!!). I still feel that if the management had not insisted on the Peace for our Time campaign, things my have turned out very different?"

Although Warm Dust never quite managed to achieve widespread acclaim in the UK, they did leave behind a legacy of three strong albums that were not only hugely popular across Europe at the time of their release but remain fondly regarded among dedicated progheads.

For years the band's albums would be highly-prized collector's items and almost impossible to find until 2001 when their first two albums were issued on CD by Red Fox Records. The third album would follow suit in 2004 when it was put out by Second Life Records.

****

Following their split the band members went their separate ways. Alan Solomon went to live in Switzerland and eventually joined Infra Steff's Red Devil Band with whom he would release two albums, I Ain't Gonna Work No More at the Gas Station (in 1979) and Average Sized an' Empty (in 1982) before joining Terry And The Hot Sox - a jive, swing and rock and roll party band that, as far as one can tell, remains a popular live act around Western Europe to this very day.

Surguy, meanwhile, rejoined Jasmin-T who changed their name to Inner Sleeve and went on to win Opportunity Knocks not once but twice in 1975, and appeared on the All Winners Show. This led to a recording contract with EMI and the release of the single Here We Go Again (written by Surguy). Having hung up his woodwind instruments to concentrate on playing steel guitar, fiddle, banjo and dobro Surguy continues to perform on the country circuit, touring Europe and doing sessions to this day.

Les Walker also remained in the music business - releasing a solo album Whatever Mood You're In in 1974, before joining Big Jim Sullivan's Tiger, with whom he would release two albums: Tiger and Going Down Laughing (both in 1976).

Although Walker returned to his native Burnley in the late 1980s, he continued to perform in the pubs and clubs across East Lancashire right up until his untimely death after a short illness on Boxing Day 2012.

Chapter Three

Following Warm Dust's split Paul found himself without a gig and facing a highly uncertain future, musically speaking. Storing his organ in his Dad's old shed (where it remained untouched for three months) Carrack settled in Camden, sharing a one-room bedsit with his girlfriend, Kathy (later his wife).

"I reluctantly got a job cleaning cars at Henley's Cars [a Jaguar dealership] for the princely sum of forty-two pence an hour," Carrack recalled. "When the initial novelty of doing 'real work' with overalls and everything wore off (after about a week) I was thoroughly miserable, apart from the fact that Kathy and I were madly in love."

While Carrack cooled his heels his former Warm Dust bandmates Tex Comer and drummer Steve Witherington had joined forces with Alan 'Bam' King (formerly of cult mod group The Action and, later, Mighty Baby) and Phil Harris to form a band called Ace Flash and the Dynamos - the sort of tongue in cheek name that was de riguer at the time.

Comer soon contacted his old mate and invited him to see the group play at Highbury Polytechnic.

"At some point [circa March 1973] I got a call from Tex Comer," Carrack reminisced. "He had met up with a couple of guitar playing songwriters from Muswell Hill, Phil Harris and Bam King, and they had formed a band with our old drummer Steve Witherington [who was soon replaced by Chico Greenwood]. They were called Ace Flash and the Dynamos [which was] a joke as they were the most uncharismatic, laid back bunch imaginable.

"They needed someone to play keys. I was that soldier. I was overjoyed at the chance to play in a band again. Not only that but Phil and Bam were also, like me, football fanatics. After an 'audition' I was invited to go with the lads to a sort of hippy commune in Cambridgeshire for the week where we were able to set up and play all night after playing football in the garden all day."

The group soon abbreviated their name to Ace, at the suggestion of Straight Music's John Curd (who had also run the independent label, Head Records, whose roster had included Mighty Baby), and soon began making a name for themselves on the burgeoning London pub rock circuit.

Over the years the phrase pub rock seems to have become something of a pejorative term. It was in fact a hugely influential movement that provided the fecund breeding ground for some of the most well-respected and enduring figures in British popular music - Ian Dury, Nick Lowe, Elvis Costello and, of course, Paul Carrack, to name but a few - and also paved the way for punk rock.

Although it's unlikely there was ever a committee to vote on such matters pub rock was a reaction to the mainstream dominated at that time in the album charts by the bloated pomp and ceremony of prog and the flash histrionics of heavy stadium rock and, in the singles charts, by glam. Eschewing as it did pretentious suites about goblins and grand viziers, week-long drum solos, collaborations with orchestras and avant-garde composers and the garish theatrics and androgyny of glam rock (a scene seemingly populated almost to a man by charlatans), the pub rock scene represented an overdue return to a back-to-basics, rootsier, good time music that didn't take itself waaaay too seriously.

"The pop business was full of these dreadful groups, Genesis and Journey and R.E.O Speedwagon and people like that," Nick Lowe recalls. "And it was all safe and run by these bean counters and know-nothings. That's why ... the pub rock thing started up. When punk came along a few years later, that was the thing that it really needed, but I would say that pub rock was spawned for the same reasons - dissatisfaction that it was all rubbish and needed to be pulled down. Because it had gotten to a point where you just couldn't have another concept album or triple bullshit thing."

Although there were those who played funk or country rock heavily influenced by The Band (such Kursaal Flyers, Chilli Willi & the Red Hot Peppers, and perhaps most notably Brinsley Schwarz which featured Nick Lowe), scene leaders like Dr. Feelgood, Kilburn & The High Roads and Ducks Deluxe played simple, honest, guitar-based rhythm and blues in the tradition of British groups like the Rolling Stones and the Yardbirds.

Pub rock's dress code reflected the back to basics approach. In stark contrast to say, the outlandish feather boas and mirrored top hats of glam, the uniform of the pub rock band was casual denim jeans and plaid shirts, often topped off with a beard or moustache. The figureheads of the movement, the largely clean shaven Dr Feelgood, were noted for their frontman Lee Brilleaux's lived-in and slept-in white suit. Bands looked menacing and dodgy, "like villains on The Sweeney" according to one journalist.

The scene itself was based primarily in London (in such notable boozers as The Tally Ho and The Hope and Anchor) and whilst this ensured it got some good press in the London-based trade papers (who erroneously promoted pub rock as 'The Next Big Thing'), it never really managed to transcend its geographical roots. Indeed Ace would be the sole exception to this rule, at least during the scene's 1972 to 1975 apogee.

"Basically we just got together to play in pubs in London like the Tally Ho and the Hope and Anchor," Carrack would later recall. "We were a bit different to most pub rock bands because we wrote a lot more of our own material, most of the other bands were playing covers, rock and roll, and we were doing a bit of that but we also wrote our own stuff and that's when I first started really writing songs."

Initially Paul played a supporting role in Ace, content merely to play his keyboards and sing the occasional song in the band's sets. "Phil Harris used to run the group," Carrack elaborated. "He was the leader and I looked up to him. I was used to being in groups and just going with the flow, but here was a guy who seemed to be in control of his own destiny. He had a bit of a plot – not ambitious, but one level up from me that's for sure."

Slowly but surely, though, as he developed his songwriting abilities it became obvious that Paul should be out front and centre.

"We started introducing songs I was writing," Paul says. "Then I eventually became the lead singer. We'd just acquired a revox and I would sit in our little place in Camden Town, and mess around with bouncing the tracks, writing songs. Then I moved again up to Muswell Hill, which was where the others lived. I was having a ball, playing the pubs with the group. We were getting the newspaper delivered and I think we might have even had a phone! That was when I wrote How Long."

Despite being one of his earliest attempts to write a song How Long would prove to be one of the best loved and most successful of his long and distinguished career.

Commonly believed to be a song about a romance on the fritz, the song was actually written about the brazen attempt by pub rock rivals Sutherland Brothers & Quiver (who included in their ranks Tim Renwick) to poach Tex Comer when their bass player, future Attraction Bruce Thomas left their ranks following a disagreement. Although Comer did guest on the Sutherlands' 1974 Beat of the Street album and played a few gigs with them he opted to remain with Ace. Within a year he would be glad he did.

Largely on the strength of How Long, which Ace had been playing live, the band caught the attention of Charisma Records' John Anthony who asked them to go on tour as an opening act for art-rockers Hawkwind. Impressed by what he saw during the tour, Anthony arranged for the group to record some demos.

On the strength of these demos Ace secured a record deal with the small Anchor label in July 1974 . Unfortunately, just as they were about to enter the studio to record their first album, Chico Greenwood left to form Baz (later to become Moonrider, who would also sign with Anchor) with ex-Tomorrow Keith West, ex-Family John Weider and Bruce Thomas and he was quickly replaced by ex-Bees Make Honey drummer Fran Byrne.

The band would record their debut - Five-A-Side - over a two-week period at the famous Rockfield Studios in Monmouth, South Wales.

"The decision to go to Rockfield was taken by the guy producing us, John Anthony," Carrack remembers. "He'd been down there with bands before... We were in the original sixteen-track studio which was a converted cowshed, I think. But we loved it there and had the time of our lives. The studio, though, looked like it was held together with bits of string. If you lent on the meter bridge of the console, then the back of the mixer fell off! But we simply had a great time. We played football all day and went into the studio to record in the evening. Well, that was the plan."

Also working at Rockfield that fortnight were Queen who were in another studio making Sheer Heart Attack. While Queen observed diligent working hours, Paul and his bandmates, it seems, were much more easily distracted.

"We were what was known as a pub rock band," Paul laughs. "We were a gigging band playing the pubs and clubs of London mostly. Basically we booked two weeks at Rockfield to make our album. We just set up our instruments and played live in the studio. To be honest, we were having too good a time in the first week to ten days. I don't think we had anything recorded that was any good.

"We played football during the day, got wrecked drinking in the evening and then maybe played a bit of music later on. Eventually John Anthony - our producer - decided to lay down the law. He was in charge of the whole thing - he was the vibe master - and we were having too much of a good old time. But for the second week, he told us to get our heads down and get something proper on record. So we knuckled down and actually recorded some good stuff. When we'd finished recording, we were pleased with every note on the five-a-side album. Plus we had the time of our lives down there for those two weeks. We did a few overdubs on the record back in London [at Trident Studios], but it was as good as finished at Rockfield.

"We just had a ball down there that first time. We were a very tight band back then. We played good music and had great times. What more could you ask for?"

If the ethos of pub rock was to make good time music then Ace manage it with deft aplomb on Five-A-Side - a highly appealing combination of laidback grooves and straight-ahead rockers, which showcased the band's tight musicianship and versatility, Carrack's developing songwriting skills and, of course, for the first time on record, his wonderful voice.

The album kicks off with the chooglin' Carrack/King composition Sniffin' About which was a fine summation of all that was good about pub rock - fine musicianship, clean sounding but twangy guitars, soulful vocals and a tight ass rhythm section. There's also a refreshing lack of pretension to the lyrics - which extol the virtues of taking it easy, hanging out and general ligging.

It's difficult not to tap your toes on this infectious little number which builds to a wonderful peak with the harmony-drenched, blissed out finale.

Paul must have been pleased with this song because it continues to pop up in his stage repertoire even to this day.

After the Phil Harris-sung Rock and Roll Runaway, a pleasant little twelve bar shuffle composed by the band comes the album's undoubted highlight - How Long.

Although it remains arguably Carrack's best known composition and almost certainly the song that changed his life, things could have been different had it been released with its original up-tempo arrangement:

"It turned out very different to how I'd originally imagined it when I wrote it," Paul explains. "When I wrote the song, I had in mind a sort of stomping Northern Soul feel and we were playing it live in that style. We actually had earmarked the song as a potential single, because we felt it was very strong. We had tried to record it earlier, during some sessions we'd had in London, so that we could use it as a single. But that didn't come off, so it was down to Wales, and Rockfield, and that's where the feel for the song really came together and it turned out different to the way I had originally envisaged. I think the version we finally came out with had a little bit more of a "late night mellow" kind of feel to it. I felt it was very strong still, but it was a little different from the first plan."

It seems incredible that the song was recorded as far back as 1974. In many ways the song has a timeless quality that defies the date of its birth, and even in 2013, it still sounds as fresh as the day it was recorded. As Carrack notes, though, the song was the game changer in his career, and even if this was the only song he ever released it would have been enough to ensure he would never have been out of work. The song was simply that good.

The soul-infused Real Feeling continues the fine start to the album and is probably the song that most resembles How Long on the album, mining a similar laid-back groove. It's interesting to note that for someone who had only recently started writing songs, on Real Feeling Carrack displays an intuitive ear for melody and song structure.

Twenty-Four Hours was another autobiographical ditty - detailing the demise of Warm Dust when Paul had been stuck in Germany without a pfennig, and waiting for the train that would take him home to the loving embrace of his lady back home. Appropriately for a track that touches on his days touring Germany with Warm Dust, Twenty Four Hours features a febrile brass section of Chris Hughes, Mick Eves and Bud Beadle which raises the song several notches above its pub rock setting.

It was clear on this song that in Phil Harris Ace possessed a lead guitarist of the highest caliber. His solo on this track reminds one of Robbie Robertson (who'd also paid his dues in the juke joints and dives of North America with Ronnie Hawkins) at his most aggressive and the fatback bass from Tex Comer shows why his band-mates were so keen not to lose him to the Sutherland Brothers and Quiver, as indeed he does throughout the entire album.

Why sees the band return to the chilled groove of How Long and Real Feeling and features some soaring harmonies by the band and another blistering solo from Harris. Although clearly not in the same league as How Long, Why might have made a decent single had it been released a few years later when the West Coast sound was at its Hotel California and Rumours driven zenith.

Time Ain't Long meanwhile was a holdover from the fag end of Carrack's Warm Dust days. Co-written with Les Walker it showed the more accessible direction his former band had been heading towards before their break-up and, as a result, fits in well with the rest of Five-A-Side.

The album's lone ballad was Know How It Feels, which sounds as though it's addressed to a former musical comrade of the band's now contemplating retirement from the music business. Although Carrack sings with great empathy on this track (ably backed by King and Harris), I prefer Ace in uptempo mode and fortunately they return to that on the next track, Satellite.

Although Satellite has only one verse and a bridge that are repeated ad infinitum Carrack does vary the melody and attack to break up the monotony; especially delightful is the way the song segues into greasy stripper routine sax outro by Chris Hughes. The playing and the harmonies are great and you can imagine this going down great at the Tally-Ho or the Hope and Anchor

The album then concludes with the Phil Harris' composition, So Sorry Baby, which settles on a pleasing soul groove with some sublime harmonies, with Byrne and Comer once again on exemplary form in the rhythm section.

Although very much of its time, Five-A-Side still stands up well today, rewarding a listen even after all these years. The musicianship and songwriting is impressive throughout and the five band members seem to have energy and enthusiasm to burn. On this showing Ace were clearly a band with a great deal of potential.

As a result the album received some very warm reviews: "This quintet with semi-pro backgrounds proves to be master of the catchy melody and the natty hook," wrote Wayne Robins in Rolling Stone magazine. " It has a benevolent addiction to lean instrumentation, seemingly well aware that virtuoso excursions would be both unnecessary and unsatisfactory. In its trenchant songwriting and engaging harmony singing, Ace emulates a number of American bands with similar virtues. Rock & Roll Runaway mimics the anguished singing of the Band, while How Long revives the Philadelphia dynamics of Hall and Oates's She's Gone. Eventually, Ace may attain the unity of vision possessed by other bands against whom it may be measured, like Steely Dan and the Eagles. Meanwhile, this is an encouraging debut with many pleasant but minor songs, and at least two, Time Ain't Long and How Long with immediate hit potential."

As the album's highlight there was no question that the album's lead single would be How Long. Although the song would turn out to be a monster hit, the initial portents were not promising, as Paul recalls: "We were driving up the M1 to a gig and there used to be a thing on Radio One called Emperor Roscoe's Round Table where they used to play the new releases and they had guests on to decide if it was going to be a hit, [well, this week] they had the Three Degrees on so we swerved over to the hard shoulder to have a listen, tuned in and they said, "Well, there's Ace with their new release How Long what do you reckon?" and they all went, "Nah, not strong enough." So we were gutted."

Irrespective of the Three Degrees seal of disapproval, Carrack knew How Long had what it took to be a big hit: "I thought it was really strong. I mean I was naive enough to think it was going to be a hit and it was but it was a very slow process. It took weeks and weeks of DJs giving it a spin as they were allowed to do in those days; they could play a bit of what they liked and it just built up word of mouth, likewise in America. It came out and it made its way very very slowly week by week all the way up the chart."

How Long would eventually peak at #20 in the U.K. charts and on the back of its success, Ace started picking up some high profile work at the BBC - appearing on Radio One's In Concert programme in January 1975 and squeezing in three Radio One studio sessions in relatively quick succession - two for John Peel (22nd October 1974 and 25th March 1975) sandwiching one for 'Whispering' Bob Harris (2nd December 1974). These recordings (which can be found on the reissues of Ace's three albums) showcase what a fine little live band Ace were and the inclusion of a cover of Marvin Gaye's Ain't That Peculiar would arguably mark the first recorded instance of Carrack's lifelong love affair with classic American soul.

Step by step Ace were climbing the ladder and in May they played their first open-air shows, opening for Yes at QPR's Loftus Road (on 10th May) and again a week later at Stoke's old Victoria Ground at which the band played How Long twice by popular demand!

If playing football grounds was a massive step up from the pub venues they'd been used to playing they were about to be propelled into another league entirely when they were invited to open for Yes throughout the North American leg of their long Relayer tour.

The timing couldn't have been more propitious for Ace to launch their assault on the United States. By the end of May 1975 How Long had climbed to #3 in the US Billboard charts and stayed there for two weeks (it was kept off the top of the charts by John Denver's Thank God I'm A Country Boy and Freddie Fender's Before the Next Teardrop Falls). Despite falling just short of the top spot How Long would prove to be a huge Stateside radio smash, as Carrack recalls: "Everywhere you went, you just couldn't get away from it."

Although their chart successes (the Five-A-Side album would climb as high as #11 on the U.S. charts, and would eventually remain the charts for an impressive twenty-two weeks while How Long's follow-up single, Rock &

Roll Runaway was also a minor hit) should have rendered them bulletproof when they supported Yes things didn't quite work out like that. Kicking off on 17th June at the Denver Coliseum and winding up on 25th July at Roosevelt Stadium, Jersey City, the tour, instead, would prove to be something of an ordeal.

Prog rockers Yes were, at that time, one of the biggest selling acts and most popular live attractions in the world. While this obviously meant Ace got the opportunity to play massive outdoor stadiums like The Hollywood Bowl, such venues and Yes's fanbase were wholly unsuited to Ace's intimate and eclectic brand of pub rock and their decidedly low-key stage show.

Having spent their career to date rarely playing anything larger than a college refectory, to find themselves suddenly playing to crowds of 25-30,000 was way out of their comfort zone.

Although Ace battled through, largely thanks to the popularity of How Long, there were occasions where the band were received with outright hostility by Yes's acolytes.

For Carrack the tour was a thankless, no-win situation: "It was a terrible billing. Our manager [Tony Demetriades - who had taken over the management reins from Phil Harris], should have been shot for putting a bar band from London in front of 15,000 Yes fans every night. I mean, we were having a blast because we were in America, and everything was new and fantastic, but we didn't know how to project or anything. We should have come over and played the grass-roots circuit. Instead it all just kind of went downhill."

At the conclusion of their American itinerary the band flew to Jamaica for a two-week working holiday and then, upon their return to England, headed straight into the studio to record the follow up to Five-A-Side. Despite their Jamaican vacation the band were in no fit state to continue their relentless schedule.

"We needed to get another album out quick, or so we were told," Carrack later explained. "And we got back to England with no material whatsoever and went straight back into the studio and tried to do it in the studio. I don't think that physically we were in any state to do that album. Really everyone was totally freaked, mentally and physically under the weather."

Ace decided their best option was to try and repeat the formula that had served them so well on Five-A- Side: reuniting with John Anthony, returning to Rockfield and even calling the album Time For Another, a clear and almost apologetic hint that the band were serving up more of the same.

"We went back to Rockfield to record that album, but it wasn't such a pleasant experience." Carrack elucidates. "That was nothing to do with the studio itself, but more to do with us as a band. We'd had this phenomenal hit in How Long and we were on the road promoting it all over the place. We were in America for around three months, touring there with prog-rock superstars Yes. And then we came under a lot of pressue to record a new album. Obviously the record company were keen to get another LP out quickly to capitalise on the success of both How Long and the album. So we had the stupid notion of going into the studio with no songs written! All we had were a few riffs and bits and pieces. That was a big mistake to make. It was the opposite of what we'd done on the first album and it really isn't the way to put a record together."

Whereas all but one song on Five-A-Side had been either written or co-written by Carrack, Time for Another saw (and suffers due to) the songwriting credits being shared more democratically: with two band compositions, presumably the result of Rockfield jam sessions (I'm A Man, Ain't Gonna Stand For This No More), two from Bam King (This Is What You Find and Does It Hurt You?), one each from Comer (Tongue Tied) and Harris (Message To You), one written by Comer, Harris and Byrne (You Can't Lose) and only three penned solely by Carrack - I Think It's Gonna Last, No Future In Your Eyes and Sail On My Brother.

Although this suggests band wanted a more equal share of the songwriting action, the reality was more prosaic. Paul himself attributes his reduced contribution on Time For Another to the fact he was going through a creative furlough caused by the success of How Long and the pressure to come with a follow-up: "I had that big smash, a bit of pressure and people looking to me for that next big smash. That kind of knocked me back a bit."

Despite his reduced input, it was Carrack's three songs that stood out. I Think It's Gonna Last was a pleasing album opener, and although it was no Sniffin' About it did at least hint at a subtle evolution in the band's direction, boasting a smoother West Coast sound - with Carrack's Fender Rhodes mixed very much to the fore - that theoretically could have gone down well on American radio.

No Future in Your Eyes meanwhile was clearly an attempt to replicate the success of How Long - with its late-night mood, harmony-rich, soul-infused groove and its accusatory lyric - and although it was another smooth piece of songcraft and was rightly chosen as the album's lead single, it worryingly failed to chart.

Sail On Brother meanwhile was a much more subdued, world-weary effort which, to be fair, matched the mood of the whole record.

Given that one of the strongest weapons on Five-A-Side had been Carrack's fine voice and songwriting, with all due respect to the other members of Ace, history has rather proved that they were not quite in his league, either as singers or songwriters, and their collective dominance of the record ultimately meant that Time for Another was nothing like as strong as its predecessor.

Admittedly, the playing is up to the same standard but there's a notably more tired ambience. The pub rock sound has been refined, polished with a smoother West Coast chamoir but the results are a tad anaesthetised, lacking the the verve and energy of Five-A-Side.

Clearly the non-stop touring was taking its toll, belied by Carrack's own rather wan expression on the cover (which shows the hirsute, casually dressed quintet sharing a round of nut-brown ales and a game of darts in their local boozer).

"I think we made a mistake with that second album," Carrack later acknowledged. "We were all disappointed with it, and we lost a bit of ground. In actual fact we should have given ourselves time and said, "It's really got to be good. If it's going to be a couple of months longer then it's going to be worth it.""

Without a single as strong as How Long to boost sales Time For Another was released to a lukewarm response and the chances of the record's success were further hampered when the band's record label fired all its promotion staff a fortnight after the album's release. Having climbed to #153 in those two weeks, the record promptly disappeared from the Top 200. For Carrack it would be an early lesson in record company caprice.

The comparative failure of Time for Another was hugely disconcerting for the band and Paul now admits that the camaraderie within the band had been affected by the relentless touring, the disastrous dates with Yes, the pressures of coping with the success of How Long and their dissatisfaction with Time for Another: "Even though for the second album we recorded in the posh new quadrangle studio at Rockfield, it wasn't the same. We just didn't have fun together as a band any more. The band dynamic was way off beam."

Although Ace were invited back to appear on BBC Radio One's In Concert programme in January 1976, it was clear their star was beginning to fade in the UK and later that month the band decamped Stateside (where they had been more successful), moving into a Spanish-style hacienda in Hidden Valley, a ranch community located in California's Conejo Valley, in the northwestern region of Greater Los Angeles.

A mere two months after arriving the band were reduced to a four-piece when Phil Harris left the band he had formed.

"It was an upset," Carrack would tell the NME. "It really was. For lots of reasons. The worst thing about it was that there was a lot that went unsaid. By the end of that second tour just before we left England we wasn't speaking a lot to each other so perhaps we should really sort it out with him as opposed to him picking up newspapers and reading things in them. Apart from the fact that it's the only thing we've got that's in the slightest worth your writing about."

The remaining members opted to struggle on.

"We were a tight little bunch of guys who'd come from nowhere," Carrack explains. "We'd had this big hit, they worked us into the ground and it went a bit pear-shaped. We got a bit burned out and there was a bit of falling out but we didn't want to give it up because we'd been through a lot together."

In June the band recruited Californian guitarist Jon Woodhead to replace Harris. Woodhead had been backing ex-Kingston Trio and composer of Daydream Believer John Stewart and had been recommended by Pete Thomas, Sheffield-born former drummer of pub rockers Chilli Willi and the Red Hot Peppers who had also been working in Stewart's band.

Although Time for Another had failed to repeat the success of Five-A-Side Carrack's personal confidence was given a boost when one of his heroes, Bobby Womack, covered How Long on his Home Is Where The Heart Is album - the first time someone else had recorded one of his songs.

****

Re-energised by the Californian sun and their new ranch lifestyle Ace headed back into the studio record their third and final album, No Strings.

Recorded at Shangri-Las Studios in Zuma Beach California and Cherokee Studios in Los Angeles with Trevor Lawrence (a late replacement for the band's original choice, Rob Fraboni), No Strings finds Ace largely leaving behind their pub rock sound and moving further into the west coast sound territory they had hinted at on Time for Another.

Happily, the experiment of democratically sharing the vocal and songwriting duties was abandoned in favour of making Carrack (who also wrote or co-wrote seven of the album's ten songs) the sole lead vocalist throughout.

It was clear that it was a more ebullient Ace this time round. Although the album's opener, Rock and Roll Singer (written by Carrack and Comer) was identifiably Ace, the addition of the world famous horn playing of Jim Price and Bobby Keyes gave the track a swagger that suggested the band meant business.

You're All that I Need, that kicks off with a riff that sounded ever so slightly like Cream's Sunshine of Your Love, was a laidback groove very much in the style of How Long. Woodhead even takes a lengthy, labyrinthine solo at virtually the same place in the song as Harris had on the earlier hit.

Side one ends with a trio of tracks - Crazy World (written by King), I'm Not Takin' It Out on You and Movin' - that sounded not unlike the polished soft rock that The Eagles were shifting by the bucketload around this time, even down to the name checks to the West Coast Highway (on the latter) and the apostrophes artfully replacing the letter 'g'. It must have all seemed a long way from the Hope and Anchor.

Side two opens with the rather delightful Gleaming in the Gloom (co-written by Bam King and the departed Harris) which boasts another wonderfully fluid guitar solo from new boy Woodhead, some lush harmonies and a particularly fine Carrack lead vocal, while the slick Let's Hang On that follows was so Southern Californian you can almost smell the orange groves.

After Comer's harmony-rich Why Did You Leave Me? the band return to their soft rock sound on Found Out the Hard Way before bringing the album and Ace's recording career to a close on the wistful and fatalistic, The Band-esque C'est La Vie, which seems to be either an open letter to a former lover (or bandmate) or a resigned summation of Ace's declining commercial fortunes.

Although No Strings sounded tailor-made for the American market of 1977, Ace had lost too much momentum to recover their former glories, which was a shame because No String represented a vast improvement on Time For Another.

You're All That I Need was rightly selected as the album's lead single in January 1977, but despite its sonic similarity to How Long and its suitability for FM radio airplay, it stiffed. Again without a solid single to attract attention to the band, No Strings could only limp to #170 in the American album charts and failed to chart at all in the UK.

Although the band put out Found Out the Hard Way as a single in the UK and flew home in May to promote it with an appearance at London's Roundhouse, Ace returned to find a very different England to the one they'd left behind. The punk and new wave era was now in full flow and although many of their pub rock friends had become bulwarks of that scene, Ace themselves were now completely out of sync with what was going on.

"The scene had changed drastically," Carrack acknowledged. "The songs I was writing were just out of time."

When a scheduled UK tour was cancelled for financial reasons the writing was on the wall and although Ace swiftly returned to the States, in July Carrack announced that he was leaving the band. Byrne, Comer and King did attempt to continue the band, ironically with John Surguy on pedal steel guitar and Les Walker on vocals but after just a couple of gigs with the new line up Ace split for good.

"I'd been getting frustrated musically and I felt I really wanted to play with different types of musicians," Paul later revealed. "I wanted to improve myself. We came back to the UK just when all the punk thing was happening and we just didn't fit in at all. We were the absolute antithesis of everything they stood for, blokes with beards and laidback attitudes who'd just mastered the art of playing on one chord for twenty minutes, and all of a sudden it was high-speed two-minute songs."

In actual fact Carrack would later admit that he thought his "career was over" at this point.

Evidently concluding that a solo career was unlikely in the punk / new wave climate Carrack instead chose to keep his head down for a while in the background as a jobbing session musician.

"That seemed to be what [my peers] did," Carrack elaborates, "and I figured that's how you progress as a musician so I started to get a few sessions playing with different people but I'm self taught so I was bluffing away like mad... so I was learning on the job."

After wetting his beak as a peripatetic gun for hire playing on German chanteuse Inga Rumpf's album My Life is a Boogie, an offer of more stable, long-term work soon arrived when Paul received a call from Glaswegian singer-songwriter Frankie Miller asking him if he wanted to work with him. Carrack, who had known Frankie since their pub rock days, was delighted to accept.

"I met him when I was in Ace at the Hope and Anchor in London," Carrack later enthused, "and I remember seeing Frankie rehearsing with a band then and he just absolutely blew me away; I thought he was fantastic."

Although his time with Miller would be brief it would coincide with the Glaswegian's most commercially successful period.

In April 1978 Carrack and Miller decamped to the The Record Plant in New York to record the Double Trouble album with producer Jack Douglas. Working alongside the pair was drummer BJ Wilson (ex-Procol Harum), Chrissie Stewart on bass, highly-rated session guitarist Ray Russell, a two-man horn section of Chris Mercer and Martin Drover and Aerosmith's Steven Tyler making several guest appearances on harmonica and backing vocals.

It was clear that Miller hadn't just hired Carrack for his keyboard skills. In fact Carrack would co-write five of the songs on Double Trouble with Miller: Love Waves, Good Time Love, The Train, (I Can't) Break Away and You'll be in my Mind.

Although the album failed to chart, mainstream success was waiting just around the corner when, in October, Miller released a cover of Darlin' (written by Q Tips brass player Stuart 'Oscar' Blandamer) which went all the way to #6 on the UK singles chart (and #1 in Norway!), which must have reminded Paul what could be achieved with a good voice and the right song.

Although Carrack (alongside Ace refugees Tex Comer and Fran Byrne) appeared on Miller's follow-up album Falling in Love (which included Darlin' and was re-titled A Perfect Fit for its American release) Paul was soon on to his next project, joining, in September 1978, art rock aristocrats Roxy Music who had reunited following a lengthy period apart.

Paul would later reveal that it was his pub rock connections that got him the gig: "I was just playing around London. I just wanted to progress as a musician and in those days all the best players around were playing sessions for various recordings, I mean that work doesn't hardly exist any more but in those days there was a lot of studio work for musicians and I saw that as a way to progress as a musician by playing with better musicians and I was playing with a band called Kokomo who were a soul outfit but the guys in that band were about the best around - bass player Alan Spenner and Neil Hubbard on guitar - and these guys did all the Bryan Ferry albums and Roxy got together to make an album and they sort of dragged me along."

Carrack would go instantly into the studio with Roxy - Bryan Ferry, Andy Mackay, Phil Manzanera, Paul Thompson and bassist newcomer Gary Tibbs (ex-Vibrators) - to record what would become their first album for three years, when it was released in March 1979, Manifesto.

For Carrack, working with Roxy meant he would have to adapt to a more meticulous way of working to the "play it live in studio" ethos to which he had been accustomed: "I enjoyed that, although it was very weird. I'd never made records like that before, where you do tons and tons of takes of these keyboard tracks with some weird effects on 'em, and then another track and another track. Roxy Music were innovators in that way of recording - taking this lick and that lick, cobbling them together to make a record."

"In a way they were kind of pioneering the way for a lot of this textured, contrived sort of stuff around today, and I thought it was funny - they did, at times, remind me of a lot of old tarts primping."

Foreshadowed by the single Trash (which peaked at #40 in the UK - Roxy's least successful single to date), Manifesto was divided into two parts - an 'East' side which featured European-influenced music and a 'West' side which featured some rather uninspired pseudo disco cuts, among them Dance Away which nevertheless peaked at #2 in the UK charts.

Although Manifesto would eventually peak at #7 in the UK album charts, reviews for the album were mixed, to say the least. Rolling Stone slated the album ("Roxy Music has not gone disco. Roxy Music has not particularly gone anywhere else either") while Melody Maker offered faint praise: "... reservations aside, this may be the first such return bout ever attempted with any degree of genuine success: a technical knockout against the odds."

While the album scaled the UK album charts Roxy embarked on a gruelling world tour which pushed Manifesto into the US Top Thirty, a market the band had previously found impossible to penetrate. Despite playing on the album they were on the road to promote, Carrack would not join Roxy on this tour - the keyboard chair being filled David Skinner.

Carrack would also lose out later in the year when he appeared to be in the running to handle the lead vocal duties on Genesis guitarist Mike Rutherford's first solo album, Smallcreep's Day. Instead the job would go to former Manfred Mann singer Noel McCalla.

"I met Mike and we had a chat," Carrack would attempt to recall many years later. "I don't think I actually auditioned for it. I can't really remember now, it's along time ago but anyway... Well, I don't know what happened there, Mike decided to use Noel who is a terrific singer."

Fortunately the next time Rutherford was in the market for a singer five years later Carrack would be the first one he called.

Following their tour Roxy completed work on a second reunion album (albeit now without drummer Paul Thompson who had left due to "musical differences") - Flesh and Blood. This time though Carrack would only appear on two tracks - playing a Solina Mellotron on Oh Yeah (which peaked at #5 on the UK singles chart) and organ on Running Wild.

Despite another round of mixed reviews ("such a shockingly bad Roxy Music record that it provokes a certain fascination" lambasted the Melody Maker who evidently didn't want to risk their new wave cred by offering props to the old guard) when it was released in May, Flesh and Blood sprinted to the top of the UK album charts (it actually topped the chart on four separate occasions).

To promote the album Roxy embarked on a European Tour, this time taking Carrack with them.

"I was ... invited to go on tour with them which was fantastic," Carrack reminisced. "I really enjoyed it because there had been a bit of a struggle after the Ace thing had fizzled out and that was back on the road in a posh way, celebrity travel and all that, lovely hotels nice people to work with."

Kicking off on 29th May 1980 in Le Mans, France the tour was dogged by misfortune. First, Paul Thompson (who had returned to the fold) broke his thumb in a motorcycle accident and had to be replaced by Andy Newmark. Ill fate then struck again when Ferry collapsed following a concert in Nice on 12th July. Doctors diagnosed a serious kidney infection and Bryan was immediately flown back to Britain for emergency treatment which caused several dates to cancelled.

Thankfully Ferry convalesced in time for a short nine-date British tour at the end of July, culminating in two shows at Wembley Arena at the start of August during which Ferry would describe Carrack, Spenner, Newmark and Hubbard as "the most expensive band in the world."

According to Carrack, there was a definite distance between the hired hands and the band: "We (the session guys) were a bit bolshie but to be honest, it was good fun and Bryan was a good laugh. He was a huge star in Europe and going on tour with Roxy was an eye opener and I really enjoyed it."

The gigs at Wembley, though, would turn out to be virtually the end of Carrack's involvement with Roxy (he would play on just one track - To Turn You On - on the band's eighth and, to date, last studio album, Avalon in 1982).

Although this period of his career had effectively established Carrack seemingly as the go to guy whenever anyone wanted a keyboard player (although Carrack would later self-effacingly claim his prolific session employment was primarily due to do with the fact that he lived near the studio in Chiswick), session work wasn't something in which he wanted to specialise indefinitely and with the punk and new wave rapidly burning itself out the time was now right for Carrack to return to his own recording career.

After signing a contract with Vertigo Records Paul would release his first solo album, Nightbird, in July 1980.

For the album (recorded at R.G. Jones Studios in London during January and February) Carrack surrounded himself with good friends such as former Ace colleague Bam King, Roxy buddies Alan Spenner, Neil Hubbard and Andy Newmark and ex-Quiver guitarist Tim Renwick (whom Carrack had obviously forgiven for trying to nick his bass player in 1974).

Although the playing throughout would be solid and slick as a result, the results are possibly a bit too smooth for my taste; there's a lack of edge and character.

That's not to say Nightbird was not without highlights. While Carrack sounds most convincing on the soulful mid-tempo cuts such as Foregone Conclusion, Love is All it Takes (which might not have sounded out of place on Michael Jackson's Off The Wall), the reggaefied cover of the Norman Whitfield and Eddie Holland penned Beauty's Only Skin Deep and The Rumour, he sounds less at ease on the more singer-songwriter efforts like There's A Good Chance, In Love with Me (written by Bam King) and the title track which closes the album. Elsewhere on the generic Bet You Never Been in Love Before and You Belong to Me there's a sense that Carrack hasn't yet quite arrived at his own uniquely identifiable sound.

In the years since the album's release Carrack has tended to dismiss Nightbird as either "bland" or "a load of dodgy love songs" and it's telling that with the exception of The Rumour's appearance on 21 Good Reasons and Beauty's Only Skin Deep on 2012's Collected, none of the tracks have ever appeared on any of Paul's Best of... compilations or live DVDs.

In the event, thanks largely to inadequate distribution, the album failed to trouble the charts.

Having failed to establish himself as a solo artist with Nightbird, Paul thus found himself looking for a new project and, as it has had a handy knack of doing throughout his career, a wonderful and exciting opportunity was just around the corner.

Chapter Four

In November 1980 UK chart favourites Squeeze parted company with their keyboard player/emcee Jools Holland. Carrack would be invited to take his place.

The core of Squeeze - Chris Difford and Glenn Tilbrook - had first joined forces in 1974 when the eighteen-year-old Difford placed a "guitarist wanted" ad in a tobacconist's window and the only person to respond was the fifteen-year-old Tilbrook. After linking up with Holland, the three formed Squeeze in the mid-1970s, with drummer Gilson Lavis and bassist Harry Kakoulli (who had been replaced by John Bentley by the time of Carrack's arrival).

Releasing their first record - their Packet Of Three EP - in 1977, Squeeze shot to fame on the back of Difford and Tilbrook's highly complementary songwriting skills. While Difford wrote the band's pithy lyrics that were as English as tuppence, in Tilbrook Squeeze possessed a tunesmith of rare skills - a composer with an unerring knack of creating highly inventive, melodic, catchy and hook-filled guitar pop. Equally complementary was their distinctive harmonic approach, which often matched Tilbrook's eternally boyish tenor with Difford's gruffer almost spoken-word style an octave below.

Backed by Lavis's consummate drumming and Holland's highly accomplished boogie-woogie piano playing Squeeze were also an enormously popular live draw.

Although the band had already released three uneven and somewhat adolescent LPs (their eponymous first, Cool for Cats and Argybargy) Squeeze had hitherto been regarded more as a two-and-a-half-minute singles act. In 1979 alone they had scored massive hits with Cool For Cats and Up The Junction (both taken from their second album) both of which reached #2 on the UK singles chart and sold a combined million copies.

I think it would be fair to say, though, that Squeeze were suffering from an image misperception prior to Carrack's arrival - their concise, energetic singles had seen the band inaccurately marketed (by their band's manager Miles Copeland) and then pigeonholed as a new wave act.

In addition with their humorous promo vids and live act dominated by the flamboyant Jools Holland, Squeeze were seen in some quarters as merely a wacky novelty act. Furthermore Difford's lyrics, excellent though they were, were very London-centric in subject matter (and often influenced by the escapades of the South London no-good-nicks who were hanging around the band at the time), and it was this parochialism that might explain why the band yet to crack America.

This was such a source of frustration for the band's co-founders that they had also recently acrimoniously and litigiously parted company with their manager Miles Copeland (Chris and Glenn feeling he'd taken his eye off

Squeeze to concentrate his time and energy on making his brother Stewart's band The Police global superstars).

"We didn't think we were achieving what we should be and we were growing frustrated with Miles," Tilbrook asserted. "There was only one hit on Argybargy [the superb Another Nail From My Heart] and it wasn't anywhere near as big as the two from the previous album. The whole situation had been drawing to a head. I think we were right to be concerned."

Following their split with Copeland (by whom Holland had opted to remain represented) Squeeze had informally hooked up with the larger than life Stiff Records co-founder Jake Riviera (who at that time also managed Elvis Costello and Nick Lowe, and would soon add Carrack to his roster), in a gentleman's agreement that Difford recalls being sealed by a handshake. They might have found a new manager but the band still had no suitable replacement for Holland, despite auditioning dozens of hopefuls, and they were on the verge of tearing their hair out. Paul Carrack, in his usual self-effacing manner, would describe himself as Squeeze's "last port of call."

"We went through about sixty keyboard players after Julian left," Difford told Creem magazine. "And we always knew that Paul was there, but we never thought of having him along for some strange reason. Then Pete Thomas [drummer of the Attractions] and our manager said, why don't you try him, so he came down and just fitted in immediately."

"I was approached by Jake Riviera, who later became my manager," Paul adds. "Jake had also taken on Squeeze. Jools Holland had left the band so they needed a keyboard player and they tried a lot of people and nobody would fit for whatever reason so Jake put me forward he said go down, have a play with the guys [and] see how it goes. So I went down. I didn't know anything about them. I was absolutely knocked out by their musicality; they were fantastic, really bright, upbeat, amazing songs, amazing players and singers and they were about to go in the studio and record an album called East Side Story and they said if you want to do it you've got the job basically.

"Now I didn't know whether I was joining the band, if I was doing the album or what I was doing but I was really just interested."

Widely reported in the press at the time, the original plan (apparently an idea suggested by Riviera) was for the East Side Story album to be a double with a side apiece produced by a dream team of Elvis Costello, Nick Lowe, Paul McCartney and Dave Edmunds.

Unfortunately for childhood Beatle nut Paul his ex-Fab Four namesake quickly dropped out of the picture and while Squeeze did record some sessions with Nick Lowe they were not fecund. In fact, the only fruit of these labours was a cover of The Valentinos' I'm Looking For a Love - featuring an excellent lead vocal from Carrack duetting with Tilbrook - which only appeared as a bonus track when East Side Story was re-issued in 1997.

While Dave Edmunds did produce the album's opening track (In Quintessence) and an early version of the song Tempted the bulk of the album would be overseen by Costello in partnership with recording engineer Roger Bechirian, who was best known for his production work for The Undertones, including the singles My Perfect Cousin and the timeless Teenage Kicks.

Having Elvis Costello (who had often championed the band and had invited Tilbrook to duet with him on From a Whisper to a Scream on his latest album, Trust) attached to the new album was a massive coup for the band. In the words of respected NME staff writer Nick Kent it was a move that would place the band "in easily identifiable league alongside Britain's finest songwriter, thus no longer trapped in someone's half-baked pre-conceptions, being dammed as another wacky, clever-clever pop group."

Costello's hectic schedule, however, meant that he was only available for a limited period of time. The record would therefore have to be made in a matter of weeks.

To ensure that their deadline was met, Costello proved something of a taskmaster, insisting that recording sessions take place from 10am until 9pm from Monday to Friday, during which trips to the pub were banned. Despite initial resistance to these conditions from Difford, the band agreed to their producer's demands.

While Carrack's presence as a new band member brought a tangible sense of freshness to the sessions (as well as another strong creative voice), Costello and Bechirian proved to be inspirational pairing behind the decks; bouncing ideas off of each other and encouraging the band to pursue some new and exciting directions, and ultimately, previously unscaled heights of artistic endeavour. The album, by unanimous approval, would be Squeeze's best yet - a sprawling, fourteen-track tour de force.

"Working with Elvis was a huge inspiration for me," the initially dubious Difford would later exclaim, "he lit my fire every day with his passion and dedication to our songs."

Whereas overdubs, studio experimentation and early synths had proliferated the band's second and third albums with veteran engineer / producer John Wood, Costello and Bechirian would adopt a no mucking about approach, which leant the album a crispness and immediacy that their earlier albums had arguably lacked.

"The album took three weeks to record whereas Argybargy took almost four months," Difford recalled with astonishment. "It was quite a shock, really. There were tracks done in the first week that were done live on the album, and usually mixed that same night."

From the album's upbeat opening track, In Quintessence, it was clear that this was a much more confident-sounding Squeeze. Based on Booker T and the MGs Time Is Tight (which allowed Carrack room to impress on the Hammond organ throughout) In Quintessence gets the album off to a particularly thumping start. Boasting a characteristically fluid guitar solo from Tilbrook and his and Difford's distinctive octave-apart vocals, there's an urgency on display here and a strong one-take feel that bubbles with vim and excitement.

Although Paul had been brought into the band as a keyboard player, it clearly made little sense for the band to ignore the fact that their new member was also a very fine singer, and he got his first chance to contribute vocals on the album's second track, Someone Else's Heart. Although Difford is the primary lead vocalist on the track (singing in a higher register than he is usually associated with), Carrack provides some fantastic harmonies with Tilbrook.

"Paul's vocals on this were fantastic," Tifford praised. "No disrespect to Jools, but it was wonderful to have someone like Paul with whom I could harmonise. Vocally it opened up an entirely different set of windows. On this song Chris sang half the verses, while Paul and I sang the other half. We did this live and it was lovely to have that vocal spread."

Piccadilly meanwhile was another of Difford's descriptive slice of working-class life vignettes and a fine example it is too. Charting the comings and goings of various Cockneys around London's busy hub Carrack shines on this track, offering some extraordinarily nimble fingered piano playing that showed how little the band missed the erstwhile Holland.

If Piccadilly was very much in keeping with Squeeze's established sound There's No Tomorrow was a radical departure from their new wave image. Costello gave Tilbrook free rein to experiment on this heady slice of Beatle-esque psychedelia and the results are quite stunning.

After the idiosyncratic, bass driven Heaven, in which Difford catalogues the salty characters hanging around some moribund after-hours drinking den (which boasts, from Tilbrook, a deliciously manic banjo solo treated to sound like a bouzouki), Squeeze turn to the yearning, feminist Woman's World, which builds to a wonderful crescendo with its staccato coda and Lavis's wonderfully Ringo-esque drum fills.

Side two begins with the effortless power pop of Is That Love, one of the most immediate songs on the album and an obvious candidate for a single release before the band take another flying leap into unknown territory with the meandering and at times disorienting F-Hole (the tale of a drunken one-night stand gone comically awry) which segues into countrified Labelled With Love - a sensitively-handled tale of a war bride who finds herself widowed and exiled in Texas after the death of her husband and returns friendless to England where she slowly sinks into debt and alcoholism.

Although Labelled With Love was an unarguably strong piece of work Elvis Costello apparently had to twist Tilbrook's arm to record it and the singer was even more resistant to its release as a single. Tilbrook, it seems, feared the band would become regarded in the eyes of the wider public as a country band.

That said, Tilbrook was in some ways guilty of failing to see the bigger picture - Labelled With Love had instant classic written all over it and it remains one of the band's best known songs, and, sadly, to date, their last UK top ten single.

While Someone Else's Bell and the quirky but catchy Mumbo Jumbo (which sounded not unlike something Costello might have recorded with the Attractions) were much more in keeping with Squeeze's established style the elegant baroque pop of Vanity Fair marked another stylistic detour. Costello made the decision to replace the band with delicate orchestration and the end results remind one of Paul McCartney's work with George Martin on such songs as Eleanor Rigby and For No One.

Incidentally, it was during the sessions for the track that everyone learned about the death of John Lennon.

"As soon as we got the news there was a deadly silence followed by us leaving for the pub," Difford recalled. "The alcohol ban went straight out the window because we couldn't possibly work in those circumstances. No one could understand why anyone would possibly want to kill John Lennon. We got all our mates like Nick Lowe to come down and got completely rat-arsed, then went back into the studio and started playing John Lennon songs."

The album closes with the rockabilly romp Messed Around, that was recorded virtually live in the studio complete with a joyous honky tonk piano break from Carrack.

"It's a breathtaking solo by Paul," Difford doffed. "Piano playing does not get any better than that. When we recorded this I felt as though I'd finally arrived, that I was in a proper band with real men."

"The song showed what a great band we had at that time," Tilbrook agreed, "one of Squeeze's strongest line-ups. East Side Story was definitely the end of our first peak. It was downhill afterwards."

The album's stand-out track, unanimously agreed upon by the band themselves, critics and the public alike was the Carrack-sung Tempted, an autobiographical song inspired by the female distractions available on tour.

"Tempted was written in a cab on the way to Heathrow," Difford disclosed. "I just wrote down what I saw and how I felt as we wormed our way through the traffic. I also must have anticipated a good time on tour as the chorus suggests."

Originally recorded during the band's sessions with Dave Edmunds, the band had never been happy with it. In fact, Tilbrook has dismissively described the early version as sounding like Jeff Lynne's "E.L.O. on a bad day" (Carrack recalls it sounding like Supertramp).

Thankfully, courtesy of Squeeze's 1996 compilation of unreleased material, Excess Moderation, we can judge the original version for ourselves. While the comparisons made by Tilbrook and Carrack both make sense, I would also add that the original sounds like the theme tune to Grange Hill!

While the tempo and chord structure are virtually identical, the drum part, instrumentation, backing vocals and, to a lesser extent, Tilbrook's vocal melody are noticeably different. With all due respect to all those involved in the making of the original version, you can understand why it was destined to gather dust.

Although it was Elvis Costello who made the call to hand the lead vocal to Carrack, this might never have happened at all had Paul not suggested a new, more soulful arrangement complete with swirling hammond organ, fatback drums and a thumping bass line from John Bentley.

"I had tried that song in about four other styles with Glenn," Roger Bechirian recalls, "none of them was quite working out. Then one morning, I arrived at the studio to find Paul trying some ideas out at the Hammond. He suggested an approach that might work, he stepped up to the mic, and the rest is history!"

"One day at the end of the album," Carrack elaborated, "we'd more or less finished everything and we were messing about and we were doing this song called Tempted which they had already recorded a different version of but we were doing it in this kind of soul soully way and I was playing the hammond organ and Elvis Costello ... came running in and he said, "this is great let's put this down," and we recorded the song in this new style and he said this is great but you know what Paul should sing it and I felt a bit strange about it because Squeeze already had two great singers, Glenn and Chris, but it's a fantastic song and I jumped at the chance to sing it."

"They had this resource in the band of Paul Carrack," Elvis Costello extolled, "and it seemed of all the songs that they had the one he could really transform. I mean privately Glenn might have thought it was a bit of a liberty for me to suggest that he didn't sing a song that he'd written."

Although he was upset at being benched on what was, after all, an obvious masterpiece, Tilbrook has always been gracious enough to acknowledge that Costello made an inspired decision and that Carrack's scintillating vocal was matchless: "Of course I was immensely disappointed and then as soon as he sang it it just had to be, it was just so right, it was great, it was so natural and I would have never ever ever have sung it like that."

It should be pointed out that Paul doesn't sing lead on the entire song. In the second verse Carrack is briefly replaced by Tilbrook and Costello (the latter in basso profundo mode).

"Paul had real difficulty getting around the lyrics of the second verse in his voice in his vocal style," Costello disclosed, "which is why the vocal arrangement idea of this crazy pseudo-Temptations arrangement [came about]. And it makes me laugh every time I hear it because I can't believe we got away with it but it has a charm because its obviously done with affection for those original records."

When the song was completed its writers knew they had a massive hit record on their hands.

"I think when we were recording the album East Side Story," Difford enthused, "Tempted stuck out like a sore thumb as being a fantastic song. And when Paul Carrack sang it, that really turned it into something brilliant. There are obvious songs like that one; when you hear them, you go, "OK, that's going to work, that's going to be really great.""

Tilbrook even considers this one of his favourite songs: "It was our first song. It was when we grew up, really, as a band. When we finished it I couldn't quite believe it was us."

East Side Story turned out to be Squeeze's finest album to date and Difford and Tilbrook have always been keen to highlight the importance of Carrack's contribution.

"Paul brought such a lot to the table," Tilbrook emphasised. "His sense of musicality is absolutely total and he can empathise with other people's ideas. I think East Side Story is our first mature album."

I personally think it remains their second best album (Carrack would also be on hand for their best over a decade later) and Costello and Bechirian deserved (and received) tremendous credit for coaxing such great performances out of the band and encouraging them to incorporate new ideas and styles without losing the essence of Squeeze's appeal.

Squeeze had never sounded as grown-up or, having largely ditched the songs about Cockney ne'er do wells (Difford wrote more or less all the lyrics whilst on tour in America), less parochial.

"That album was great fun to make, and the band were great to work with," Roger Bechirian later reminisced. "It was also fun between me and Elvis. We would come up with ideas and just push them into doing what we wanted! Squeeze were used to working for months on their albums, and I wanted to work fast, and spontaneously on this one. We had one run-through with song choices with the band, in a rehearsal studio, then straight into the studio! I'm not sure they trusted us at first, but then Glenn became really excited about the whole thing."

The band were equally pleased with the way everything had panned out after the turmoil of their splits with Holland and Copeland.

"Moving to Riviera Global was like moving to a larger gang," Difford reflected. "Squeeze used to call ourselves "The Blob," five people moving around together, chained invisibly at the hip. When we joined Riviera Global we were part of a bigger blob with Elvis and his band, Nick Lowe and Dave Edmunds. It was a great community of hearts and minds and a very exciting time."

Having completed the album Squeeze had a chance to continue to be a part of that hive mind when they hit the road in the New Year, supporting Elvis Costello and the Attractions on their 'English Mugs and Their Old Chinas Squeeze Tour' of North America. Starting in Vancouver the two groups would play twenty-nine dates in a little over a month before the tour came to a close in Toronto on 9th February 1981.

For Carrack the tour would be one of the biggest challenges of his career to date: "When I joined Squeeze, it was just before East Side Story, so my initiation was to invent the parts for these new songs. I got a nudge here and there, but it was basically left up to me to come up with the keyboard parts. When it came to touring, it was pretty hectic; I was cramming the records, learning all the changes. If the parts were obviously integral to the song, I would cop them. But I wouldn't say I played the whole catalogue verbatim. To be honest, it was a real kick up the ass when I joined the band. Maybe I felt a little over my head to start with, but it certainly got my chops together. Their songs change all over the place! Up until that time, a lot of the music I'd been involved in was a different kettle of fish."

It says much for Carrack's musicianship that no-one noticed his struggles. Indeed these first shows without Holland were greeted with tremendous enthusiasm by the press, with leading US trade journal Billboard magazine complimenting, "the band's greater onstage confidence," and their "maturation into an act less reliant on its its quirky between songs patter and occasional theatrics."

"Departed keyboard player Jools Holland," Billboard continued, "largely dominated the concert image of the band with his arch remarks and antic mugging to charm some concert goers while leading others to believe Squeeze itself was anything but serious. If Difford and Tilbrook remain gracious about their old partner, it's clear they're even more enthusiastic about his replacement Paul Carrack."

"Now that we've been together this long," Difford told the magazine, "you'll find that the new tracks have taken more of a keyboard grip. He's definitely taking a strong role."

"It's impressive that Paul has become established with this band so fast," added Tilbrook. "Now people don't need to refer back to Ace."

At the end of the tour Tilbrook could barely contain his enthusiasm about Squeeze's new line-up: "That tour was the best we've ever been involved in. Period. The venues were well-chosen, the itinerary was well worked out and both bands complemented each other well enough for us to actually realise that at last, yes, we could quite conceivably be very big in the States."

Upon his return to the UK Carrack dipped his toe back into the world of session work, adding keyboard and piano overdubs to The Undertones' third album, Positive Touch (produced by Roger Bechirian), before rejoining his Squeeze colleagues to promote East Side Story which was finally released on 15th May to widespread critical acclaim.

Rolling Stone even went so far as to label Difford and Tilbrook the "new Lennon & McCartney" (which, after the quote was milked by the A&M press office, became something of a cross to bear for the two songwriters).

To promote their masterpiece Squeeze hit the road with something of a vengeance. Indeed from May to August there barely seemed a night when Squeeze weren't on stage.

After kicking off the tour on 8th May at Manchester University, a week later the BBC recorded the band at the Oxford Polytechnic for their In Concert programme, a broadcast that would underline why Tilbrook was so enamoured with this line-up of the band, and also how effortlessly Carrack had become integrated within it. It's also interesting to note that Paul was allotted two more lead vocals throughout the set: as well as Tempted he would also take the lead on Out of Touch (a new song written by Difford and Tilbrook) and sang co-lead (with Tilbrook) on Too Many Teardrops, a song written by Nick Lowe and his wife Carlene Carter.

Towards the end of June Squeeze's tour moved to North America, playing thirty-three dates between 25th June and 8th August.

Ahead of the US leg of tour Tempted was selected as the first single from the album to be released Stateside.

"I was excited but a little embarrassed when the song was chosen as a single," Paul confessed, "and actually became the band's first hit. The band had been knocking on the door for several years making great records and it must have been difficult for Glenn to have the new boy come in and take the credit but if he was put out he hid it very well. Far better than I could have done had the shoe been on the other foot."

Buoyed by American FM radio play (and, in the nascent days of MTV, a promo video featuring three women gyrating gratuitously at the side of the stage as the band performs), Tempted came close to cracking the American Top 40.

Although it would only peak at #49 on the Billboard Hot 100 it did reach #8 on the Billboard Mainstream Rock Chart. Although it's surprising that it didn't reach a higher chart placing (blamed in part by Difford on their record label A&M's failure to throw the full heft of their promotional might behind the band), it was still Squeeze's biggest stateside hit to date and ensured that whenever it was sung in concert it would be greeted with a rapturous reception.

At the conclusion of their North American perambulations Squeeze returned to England to conclude their tour at the Nottingham Playhouse on 15th August. The Playhouse gig, though, would be Carrack's farewell appearance with Squeeze (at least for the foreseeable future) and a fortnight later his departure was announced to the press.

"It's difficult to understand why, when things are going so well," Difford sighed to the NME. "It's funny. I think that around this time of year Squeeze are like a football team with people moving on to different clubs. You could say that Paul was offered large amounts of money by an outfit operating in the Acton area [named in the article as Carlene Carter and her band, the CC Riders, who were at that time working on a new album with Carlene's husband Nick Lowe]."

Although Carrack had been quickly established himself as an indispensable member of Squeeze, and Difford and Tilbrook could hardly be accused of hiding his light under a bushel, it was clear that there would be little or no room for his songwriting in Squeeze - which effectively existed as a two-man duopoly, a fact acknowledged by both Difford and Tilbrook, and one that Carrack, to be fair, had no wish to break.

"Squeeze had an established identity largely through the singing and songwriting of Glen and Chris and I had no desire to upset that," Carrack confirms. "However I still harboured desires to be more than just a keyboard player, much as I enjoyed being in the band."

Carrack had also been encouraged in his decision to leave Squeeze by his new manager - Jake Riviera, with whom the band (primarily at Tilbrook's instigation) had refused to sign a contract earlier in the year.

"Jake persuaded me that it wasn't in my best interests to stay with Squeeze," Carrack elaborates, "because I would always just be a sideman and I was happy being a sideman in the band because I didn't want to ingratiate myself, because the identity of the band was the songs and the singers so I was just along for the ride but Jake said you know it's not good for you to stay there too long so I was with them for about a year so I then left in order to work more with Nick Lowe."

Although Carrack left Squeeze with the best wishes of the band, who no doubt understood his rationale, Squeeze's mainmen were gutted to lose such a valuable asset.

"It was very upsetting to the band when Paul left," admitted Tilbrook (who once described Carrack as "one of the loveliest men ever in music"). "As football pundits say, no disrespect to Don Snow [Carrack's replacement], but the chemistry within the band and our relationships changed dramatically."

"He put a trademark on Squeeze which still lives to this day," added Difford in 2012, "and that's a really gracious thing and a loving thing for him to have done as its not often you get someone with such talent and such soul come into your band give you a great song and then leave the band."

In some ways Carrack's decision to abandon Squeeze must have raised eyebrows, given that he appeared to be swapping a supporting role with one band for a not too dissimilar role with another. In addition, having just scored their breakthrough hit in America and with Labelled With Love heading for the the UK top ten in October, one could argue that, as 1982 approached, Squeeze seemed poised for long-term chart success while it's fair to say that Nick Lowe, despite being in my view one of England's national treasures, was approaching a downward curve commercially. The main sop for Paul though was that working with Nick Lowe would enable him to make another solo album.

"There wasn't any money involved [being in Squeeze];" Carrack would reason, "it was purely a labour of love really. But at the same time, I realised it wasn't exactly what I wanted to do. This is something that seems to be difficult for people to comprehend, that I can be in a group and give them my all, but at the same time know what I wanted to do was somewhere else. There were times after I did quit when I thought it was a crazy thing to do. But at the time, there were other things in the cards. I wanted to play with Nick. I wanted to do my own record. And I couldn't do it all."

Lowe and Carrack had been friends from their days on the London pub rock circuit, when Paul was fronting Ace and Nick Lowe was the primary songwriter and vocalist in Brinsley Schwarz.

Although the Brinsleys had been widely acclaimed critically and had recorded six albums for United Artists over their course of their career, none of them, as was typical of pub rock bands, had been commercially successful.

Following Brinsley Schwarz's demise in 1975, Lowe went solo and eventually signed to seminal punk / new wave label Stiff Records founded by Jake Riviera (who had been a roadie for Chilli Willi and the Red Hot Peppers) and Irish impresario and former Brinsley Schwarz manager Dave Robinson (the label, trivia fans, was started thanks to a £400 loan from Dr. Feelgood frontman Lee Brilleaux).

In August 1976 Lowe released the marvellous So It Goes b/w Heart of The City, the first single on the Stiff Records label, and shortly afterwards produced the The Damned's eponymous first album which included New Rose which is widely regarded as being the United Kingdom's first punk single (the seven-inch was released in November 1976).

Following his success with The Damned, Lowe effectively became Stiff's in-house producer cum A&R man. It was Lowe, for example, who added the young Elvis Costello to the Stiff roster. Stiff's head honchos bafflingly originally intended to sign Costello merely as a staff writer. Fortunately Lowe's championing of Costello "convinced them we should sign him as an artist, not just a writer."

When the combustible Robinson and Riviera axis split in early 1978 after a series of disagreements, Riviera left Stiff in early 1978 to form the short-lived Radar Records, taking Costello and Lowe with him as a settlement package.

The move to Radar marked the start of a hectic period for Lowe. In March 1978 he released his acclaimed debut album, Jesus of Cool (renamed Pure Pop for Now People in the US) which spawned the top ten single I Love the Sound of Breaking Glass.

The Jesus of Cool's album cover told you everything you needed to know about Lowe before you even put the record on the turntable. Waggishly posing as six different rock star archetypes (among them a denim-clad troubadour, a plaid-bedecked pub rocker, a beatifically stoned hippy and a double-necked guitar-toting muso) Lowe promised versatility and music with a sense of humour.

There was always something singular about Lowe in the cut and thrust of the new wave. Whereas the likes of Costello and Parker were 'Angry Young Men' with a deeply political edge to their work, Lowe appeared rakish and insouciant, and saw the funny side of the rock and roll game. Refreshingly, like Carrack, the last thing you could accuse Lowe of was taking himself too seriously.

In fact Lowe's lyrics were so full of sardonic wit and satire that Rolling Stone magazine sarcastically described Pure Pop as "a novelty record."

Raffish and charming and someone upon whom the rock press could always rely for a pithy soundbite Lowe's profile could hardly have been any higher during the late seventies.

"Round about the end of the 1970s, for a short and glorious time," Lowe would later recall fondly, "we were the monkeys in the wheelhouse."

Fondly known by his peers as 'Basher' which reflected his supposed "bash it out now, we'll tart it up later" approach in the recording studio, Lowe produced the first five studio albums by Elvis Costello & The Attractions, the first and third albums by Graham Parker & The Rumour (which included Lowe's former band mates, Bob Andrews and Brinsley Schwarz), Clover, Wreckless Eric, The Pretenders' 1978 debut seven-inch Stop Your Sobbing, and Dr. Feelgood's 1977 album Be Seeing You, as well as co-writing (with Gypie Mayo) the Feelgood's Milk and Alcohol which reached the UK Top 10 in 1978.

As well as writing and producing hits for other acts he also would also continue to score them himself, such as Cracking Up and the timeless Cruel to Be Kind (which peaked at #12 on both sides of the Atlantic) which were both taken off his second solo album Labour of Lust which marked the start of his collaboration with Rockpile, the quartet he co-led with legendary Welsh producer-guitarist Dave Edmunds.

Noted for their strong rockabilly Rockpile had been an interesting experiment and a popular one on both sides of the Atlantic. Ably assisted by guitarist Billy Bremner and drummer Terry Williams, Rockpile essentially served as the backing band both in the studio and on the road for its two leaders depending upon who had an album to record and subsequently promote. They were also studio guns for hire, backing country singer Carlene Carter (daughter of June Carter and Johnny Cash's stepdaughter - whom Lowe would marry in August 1979) on most of her 1980 album Musical Shapes and Stiff act Mickey Jupp on side one of his Stiff album Juppanese.

Although Rockpile had fizzled out in somewhat acrimonious circumstances, Nick Lowe was clearly suggesting to Paul that they could form a similar alliance. Joining them would be guitarist Martin Belmont (who had been in pub rock act Ducks Deluxe, Graham Parker's Rumour and, more recently, as a guest of Elvis Costello's Attractions on the English Mugs tour), drummer Bobby Irwin (formerly of Stiff act The Sinceros) and bassist James Eller.

Although Carrack had left Squeeze to work with Lowe, it was his wife Carlene Carter with whom he would work first. Famous not only as the daughter of her legendary parents, Carlene was a prolific songwriter and a great singer in her own right, although her fame had yet to translate into widespread commercial success.

Carrack would join his new colleagues at Nick Lowe's Ampro Studio (in reality the converted living room of Nick and Carlene's large terraced house in Shepherd's Bush) to work on Carter's fourth solo album, Blue Nun (an R & B-influenced Europe-only release produced by Nick).

Just as Elvis Costello had realised during East Side Story when you had a voice as good as Paul's at your disposal it made sense to put it to good use. As a result Paul would duet with Carlene on Edwin Starr's gospel-tinged Oh How Happy and the album's highlight and lead single Do Me Lover (that Mr and Mrs Lowe had written with Paul specifically in mind).

Despite the disappointing reaction of her American label who refused to sanction a Stateside release, Blue Nun is a good little album, well worth tracking down, particularly the re-issue which features a third Carter / Carrack duet on a cover of Creedence Clearwater Revival's Born to Move (which for some reason was re-named C'mon Feets).

Following the completion of Blue Nun (and a short promotional trip to Europe), Lowe swooped to poach his wife's band.

"They were all bloody out of work! Bunch of fucking scoundrels," Lowe would joke. "They were playing with Carlene on some gigs; when she stopped I just swung in and picked them up."

Christened The Chaps (before quickly being re-branded as Noise to Go) the new band immediately set about helping finish Lowe's fourth solo album Nick the Knife.

Continuing the format he had established on Jesus of Cool, Lowe runs a highly eclectic gamut of styles on Nick the Knife - low-fi garage thrash on Stick it Where the Sun Don't Shine, ersatz reggae on his remake of Rockpile's Heart, country-soul on Too Many Teardrops, rockabilly on Burning, unabashed country and western on Couldn't Love You Anymore Than I Do, funky Jackson Five flavours on Let Me Kiss Ya and 1950s doo wop pastiche on Ba Doom.

The album would include a number of my favourite Lowe songs - the effortlessly brilliant My Heart Hurts, the swampy One's Too Many (And A Hundred Ain't Enough), the witty Queen of Sheba and the excellent unabashed Tamla Motown tribute Raining, Raining (that Carrack would later record on his Old, New, Borrowed and Blue album in 2007).

The album in the can, for release in February 1982 (it eventually peaked at #50 on the Billboard Top 200 and #99 on the UK album charts) Nick Lowe and his Noise to Go were soon on the road - supporting The Cars on a seven-week tour of the US, kicking off in Philadelphia on 8th February 1982 and winding up in Largo, Maryland on 22nd March.

Upon their return to the UK Noise to Go performed some shows in the UK, one of which, at the Hammersmith Palais, was recorded by the BBC for broadcast on Richard Skinner's Rock Hour show in June. The broadcast captured the band in electrifying form on a set that included three spoilers from Carrack's soon to be completed second solo album - Suburban Voodoo - recorded at Lowe and Carrack's old haunt, Rockfield Studios.

The album would be engineered by Rockfield's in-house specialist Paul Cobbold who recalls a lovely story that perfectly illustrates Carrack lack of rock star vanity.

Since both men were known by the same nickname, whenever someone called out "PC," both men would answer. To put an end to the confusion, Carrack came up with an endearing solution.

"He was very gracious," Cobbold cherished. "He simply looked at me and said, "To make matters easier I'll relinquish the name. From now on you're PC, I'll just be Carrack! It's stuck ever since. He was a great guy to work with and so talented."

After the disappointing sales of Nightbird there was a lot riding on Suburban Voodoo if Carrack wanted to establish himself at last as a bona fide solo artist and Lessons in Love gets the album off to a suitably punchy and auspicious start. Following a twangy intro worthy of Steve Cropper the song unfolds into a catchy organ-driven stomper.

What is great about Lessons in Love, and indeed the entire album is Lowe's decision to keep things simple - all the songs use a flab-free guitar-bass-drums-keyboards line-up and there's a refreshing lack of overdubs. Credit must be given to the band (in which Carrack's Hammond is front and centre) which sounds a great deal hipper and harder rocking than the proficient but rather anonymous-sounding session men Paul had hired on Nightbird. Furthermore the decision to ignore synthetic sounds made for an album that has thankfully barely dated a lick.

The breezy radio-friendly Always Better With You continued the album's fine start. With its singalong chorus and jangling guitars this could have been a sizeable hit for someone with a higher profile at that time. Although written solely by Carrack, there's a breezy Nick Lowe quality to this track with a Beatley middle eight and an especially fine chorus.

With its craven nod to The Temptations' My Girl bass intro, classic Motown was clearly what Carrack was aiming for on the exceptional I Need You, and Carrack and Lowe show their mastery of the form with aplomb. The song with its simple but affecting sentiments was perfect for Paul's soulful voice while Carrack's co-writers Belmont and Lowe provide some nice Tamla "oohs" and "sha-la-las" throughout as well.

I Need You deserves its place on any Paul Carrack Best of Compilation and also deservedly became a top forty hit on the Billboard Hot 100 (bizarrely released as a one-sided single - a brief innovation by CBS). One thing that strikes one instantly is the sincerity Carrack evinces, which one journalist remarked "stood out like a sore thumb alongside his compulsively ironic colleagues."

"He's a soulful cat," his producer would later commend, "people can see that, they can sense it, that he's soulful. He has the ability to make people see that he is being truthful and he's not a fraud. Pop music is filled with frauds and actually some of the frauds are quite entertaining but look at the length of his career. You really don't stick around that long if you haven't got something really special going for you and he's a really great musician."

Carrack proves what a great musician he is on the album's fourth song, I'm In Love (co-written by Carrack and Carlene Carter). Again kicked off with a twangy Stevie Cropper guitar lick, the band rock on this track, with drummer Bobby Irwin whacking his snares like a man possessed and Martin Belmont riffing superbly throughout. Carrack joins the party with one of his best vocals on the album, one that any of his soul heroes would have been proud to claim as their own.

If Don't Give My Heart a Break sounds more like a Nick Lowe song, it should as he co-wrote it with wife Carlene (who recorded her own version of the song on her C'est Bon album). Not surprisingly this is a more country-tinged offering which allows Carrack to show his versatility. Especially enjoyable is Carrack's raw and gutsy vocal towards the end of the song which shows he could belt it out with the best of them.

Another keeper though was the Carrack-penned A Little Unkind, one of my favourites on the album. The song barrels along at a fair old lick, embellished by some staccato Motown guitar stabs from Belmont and some amazing organ and piano playing and another heartfelt vocal from Paul. As the song was not too dissimilar in arrangement to the cover of You Can't Hurry Love that Phil Collins would take to the top of the UK charts later in the year it's rather criminal that A Little Unkind didn't reach a wider audience.

Side two kicks off with the funky Out of Touch, Carrack's parting gift from Difford and Tilbrook (Squeeze included it as the opening track of their Sweets from a Stranger album).

Bearing all the quirky hallmarks of a Tilbrook composition and Difford's scalpel sharp wit the song was a glove fit for Carrack who delivers another exemplary vocal and the band smoothly navigate their way through the tricky arrangement.

What a Way to Go (written by Carrack with Belmont, Lowe and James Eller) was another fine pub rock / blue-eyed soul hybrid, with its rolling organ, witty lyrical couplets and tight arrangement this was good time music at its best. Paul's gutsy vocals and his playing really shine on this track offering not only lashings of organ but a wonderful boogie-woogie piano solo to boot.

So Right, So Wrong was another candidate for a single with its infectious call and response chorus. The track finds Paul at the upper limits of his register, which has the happy consequence of showing there's plenty of grit in his usually more honeyed vocal cords. Co-written with his Noise to Go bandmates Carrack again displays shows his effortless ability to create authentic soul tunes. His eyes might have been the proverbial blue but Sam and Dave would have been proud to have released this in their pomp and it remains one of my all time favourite Carrack songs.

Another highlight was the Nick Lowe-penned From Now On. The song had future standard written all over it and merited a slew of cover versions. It was a generous move on Lowe's part to part with such a gem, as it was one of the best songs he'd written in years. "Paul," Lowe explained, "sounds best when he's singing songs that aren't of any consequence lyrically. I can write for him quite convincingly, but I'm not so good at sounding convincing at performing these songs myself."

It seems strange however that Paul didn't choose to close the album with it because the two actual closing cuts are, at least for me, slightly anti-climactic as a result. Call Me Tonight (co-written by Paul with Alan Spenner) is a more generic workout redeemed by some impassioned lead vocals and a dazzling piano break while I Found Love (written by Neil Hubbard) finds Paul in Hall and Oates territory, with a more slick eighties production sound than elsewhere on the record.

Though largely ignored in the UK, the album was a massive critical success in the US when it was released in August 1982. The highly influential Rolling Stone magazine, for example, gave the album a four-star review and later named it as one of their Top Twenty Albums of the Year, all of which represented a stunning comeback for someone who hadn't had a hit record for several years (Tempted aside).

The Stateside success of Suburban Voodoo was no fluke in a quiet year; with its wide cross-over appeal and radio-friendly contents the album was a highly impressive effort containing more potential singles than most people manage in an entire career.

Of course Nick Lowe deserves credit not only for his sympathetic and spontaneous-sounding production which allowed Carrack to shine throughout, but also for generously co-writing six of the tracks and Noise to Go deserve equal praise for their versatility in adapting their pub rock chops to blend in with Carrack's more soulful sound.

Strangely Carrack himself has occasionally been slightly dismissive of his sophomore effort: "Suburban Voodoo ... is quite interesting if you listen to it now. I can manage about three tracks and then I have to go and have a lie down as its quite fuelled." Personally, I think that's part of its enduring charm.

While it is strange that Suburban Voodoo didn't make him the poster boy for blue-eyed soul, for Carrack it had all been a matter of bad timing: "Later it was observed that my album may have been released prematurely, that it predated a trend. If it'd come out a year later, when Paul Young and Boy George were happening in a similar vein, it might have stood a better chance. But I've never been interested in being a 'flavor of a week.' I figure that sooner or later, people will figure it out if you've got something good to offer. Still, I'm not sure if getting a hit record is, ultimately, a question of timing or pure luck."

After a short US tour to promote Suburban Voodoo in September and October (billed as Paul Carrack's Noise to Go featuring Nick Lowe), Carrack's solo career would again be placed in storage, this time for five years.

Chapter Five

The start of 1983 saw Noise to Go embark on another mammoth trek up and down America, supporting Tom Petty and the Heartbreakers on their Long After Dark Tour. Beginning on 17th January in Fresno, California the tour would not wind up until 25th April, with Carrack and Lowe squeezing in some club dates on their days off.

Returning home the offers of work kept on coming for Carrack and the spring would see him laying down keyboards on The Pretenders' single Thin Line Between Love and Hate (from their third album Learning to Crawl) and playing organ on The Smiths' eponymous debut album (Carrack would appear on Reel Around the Fountain, I Don't Owe You Anything and You've Got Everything Now), another aspect of his vast curriculum vitae that often seems to take people by surprise.

"I got a call from John Porter [whom Paul had known from his Roxy Music days] who said he was producing this new band who were "a bit different" who had this big cult following," Carrack recalls. "He sent me round some demos to give me a clue what it was about but I wasn't sure what to make of it.

"I turned up at the studio to overdub a bit of organ on two or three tracks. I was introduced to Johnny Marr who struck me as being a really nice young lad. I remember Morrissey brooding away in the corner of the control room. I assumed he was shy as he didn't come over. He looked an unlikely rock star at the time with the horn-rimmed glasses. I did some 'dubs with no fuss and Morrissey passed his comments to me through John. The one thing he did say to me was that one of my Hammond overdubs sounded like, "Reg Dixon on acid," which I took to be a good thing."

"Obviously they must have liked what I did because it stayed on the album so it's quite a feather in my cap. I had my one of my boys came home from college one day and he said, "Hey dad, did you record on The Smiths?" and I said, "Yeah," [so] I went up quite a few notches in his estimation at that point."

Many years later The Smiths' bassist Andy Rourke would be highly complimentary about Paul's contribution to the record, telling Select Magazine, "John Porter suggested getting that bloke Paul Carrack in on keyboards to see what would happen, and I thought it really brought it alive."

After moonlighting with The Pretenders and The Smiths, Carrack returned dutifully to Noise to Go (now rechristened The Cowboy Outfit following James Eller's departure - Nick Lowe took over the bass duties) who were about to embark on yet another intensive period of recording, working on John Hiatt's Riding With The King LP and Lowe's The Abominable Showman.

The Cowboy Outfit would back the widely respected American singer-songwriter on the second side of his album (Ron Nagle & Scott Matthews produced the first side, Lowe the second) and are in fine form throughout, effortlessly complementing Hiatt's bluesy voice.

Carrack's contributions were particularly effective, offering his distinctive organ riffs to the title track (that was later covered by B.B. King and Eric Clapton on their album of the same name after Hiatt reworked the lyrics) and some superb piano playing to the epic, outstanding Book Lovers.

The record belongs in any serious music fan's collection and certainly Hiatt was pleased with it: "I always kind of look at Riding with the King as the first album where I really put it altogether. I finally figured out what I was all about and found three or four styles I liked to work in."

Following on from the supremely high quality of Riding With the King it's frustrating that Lowe failed to find the inspiration to respond with an album equally as strong.

In fact, The Abominable Showman is widely regarded as the nadir of Lowe's career. This is perhaps a trifle harsh, filled as it is with a decent quota of hooks, The Cowboy Outfit's solid musicianship, Lowe's winning voice and, as usual, a wide palette of styles.

The album is fast out of the blocks with the one-two punch of We Want Action and the superb Ragin' Eyes (on which Paul's exemplary honky-tonk keyboard work is much to the fore). With its amusing lyrics, infectious melody and inventive performances from the entire band, Ragin' Eyes is an absolute gem. Incidentally when it was released as a single (which inexplicably failed to chart) it came complete with wacky promo vid which captures Carrack sporting some razor sharp mutton chops and yellow winkle pickers!

After this bright start the ersatz calypso reggae of Cool Reaction is less effective and suffers from its sheen of 1980s studio ticks, which is surprising given Lowe's reputation for authenticity, rootsiness and good taste. Likewise the puntastic Time Wounds All Heels (co-written by Simon Climie) appears to find Nick in an ill-conceived and ultimately fruitless pursuit of another big chart hit and is ruined by some rather intrusive female backing vocals. In fact the song sounds precisely like the sort of anodyne pop that the song's co-writer would score hits with a few years later with Climie Fisher.

Things pick up on the pro-woman and Costello-esque Man of a Fool with some particularly fine organ playing from Carrack but then the first side of the album closes on a disappointing note with the throwaway surfer-pastiche-cum-doo-wop of Tanque-Rae.

For Carrack fans the album's highlight though would be the infectious Wish You Were Here, on which Paul shares lead vocals with Lowe. With its contemporary pop soul feel Wish You Were Here could have been an outtake from Suburban Voodoo and although the song was released as a single in the US, it bafflingly failed to chart.

Wish You Were Here was followed by Chicken and Feathers, a decent song but one that again finds Nick in uncertain and uncharacteristic territory, dousing the production in some now very dated studio touches: echo on the vocals, de riguer spanish guitar interjections, those irritating female backing vocals again and those cheesy eighties synths that 'Basher,' I'd wager, would never have allowed on John Hiatt's record, for example.

Chicken and Feathers is followed by the pretty but forgettable soul ballad Paid The Price (which a Carrack vocal might have enlivened) before the album finishes strongly with the slight but enjoyable rockabilly of Saint Beneath The Paint and the jazzy torch song How Do You Talk to an Angel which pointed the way to Lowe's creative renaissance on his Brentford Trilogy in the 1990s.

While the sheer eclecticism of his songwriting is something I've always admired many critcs appeared to enjoy using this as a stick with which to beat Lowe, describing the album as "confused" (critics, it seemed, were either expecting Lowe to pick one genre and stick with it or come up with a dozen variations on I Love the Sound of Breaking Glass).

In addition to the negative reviews, it was also clear that Lowe and his band were swimming increasingly against the tide commercially and sales of The Abominable Showman were poor, stalling at #129 on the US album charts.

Although their records weren't selling Lowe and Carrack remained a popular live attraction and in November they teamed up with Hiatt for a short European tour where German radio was on hand to record one of their shows for posterity. What is interesting about Carrack's showcases is that he appeared to be moving away from the material on Suburban Voodoo, choosing to perform only I Need You and Lesson in Love among his seven allotted songs. Instead Carrack would perform two new compositions, Soul Cruisin' and I Can't Win With Your Love and a cover of Little By Little (in addition to old standbys Tempted and How Long).

If the new material suggested Paul was building up to another solo record it didn't materialise as he would be dropped by his record label. Carrack did shop around for a new deal but there were no takers.

"After making what I thought was a really good record," Carrack bemoaned, "with a hit single, it was a bit of a blow to be dropped by CBS/Epic. But we struggled on, making our demos. I think that those demos, being raw and having that Nick Lowe production, made it harder at the time to get me a deal."

Carrack also later confessed that the people he had collaborated with in the early 1980s had knocked his songwriting confidence: "When I was involved with Squeeze and we were under the same roof as artists like Elvis Costello and Nick Lowe, I knew that my lovey-dovey, simple, heartfelt lyrics just weren't up to that sort of standard. They were in a different league. That made me a bit insecure about the writing. Those guys were always great. It's lyrics we're talking about. They have an angle on stuff and some original thought, whereas I'm 'a moon in June' guy, let's be honest ... it was hard living in the shadow of Nick, Glenn, Chris, Elvis etc..."

****

With his solo career effectively on hold Carrack continued to work as a gun for hire and his next port of call would be to join Madness for a brief spell. The much-loved 'Nutty Boys' had racked up dozens of ska-influenced hits during the late 1970s and early 1980s and were without doubt the most successful singles act of this era in the UK.

The start of 1984, however, saw the band in a state of flux. They were in the middle of attempting to move to a more mature sound and had recently parted company with Mike Barson, their keyboard player and most prolific songwriter.

When Carrack was invited to replace Barson he had to admit that he didn't own any Madness records. A complete set was quickly couriered to his home and after an intensive two weeks learning their songs he was ready to join the band.

After appearing on The Tube (hosted by Jools Holland) to perform their new single, Michael Caine, Carrack and his new bandmates flew to Los Angeles on 19th February to promote their Keep Moving album.

The trip would include some live dates in Los Angeles, San Francisco and San Diego (during which the Nutty Boys persuaded Carrack to sing a solo version of Tempted as an encore, which went down a storm with concertgoers) as well as a number of radio and TV appearances - including an appearance on 3rd March on the prestigious Dick Clark's American Bandstand show.

After performing Keep Moving and The Sun and the Rain the appearance on Bandstand rapidly descended into farce with wacky sax player Lee Thompson seemingly hell-bent on pinching the august host's backside. Having accomplished his juvenile aim the clearly rattled presenter asked, "Have you no respect?" An inscrutable Carrack wisely kept his counsel behind his keyboard throughout.

Although helping out Madness was never intended to be a long-term arrangement, Paul would always just about remember his time with the Nutty Boys with tremendous affection: "I ... remember spending an amazing night in town after playing keyboards with Madness on The Tube. The next thing I knew was waking up on a plane to the USA where I spent the next few months touring with them. I was in my thirties and they were hardly out of their teens but I wouldn't have missed it or any other part of my career for anything."

58

Upon his return to the UK Carrack again returned to the Cowboy Outfit who were ready to hit the road again to promote their new album - Nick Lowe and His Cowboy Outfit - recorded in January and released in May.

After the disappointment of The Abominable Showman, Cowboy Outfit was a much welcome return to form.

Abandoning the dodgy production embellishments and the poppier fluff that had littered Showman Lowe actually sounds like he's put a bit of effort into this record. Even the cover shows the bandleader hitching up the slacks of his zoot suit like he means business (Lowe rather compromises this, however, by looking louche and smoking a fag).

The album hits the ground running with the breathless Tex-Mex flavoured Half a Boy and Half a Man - the sort of track that shows why everyone should be a fan of Nick Lowe or at least own a career-spanning anthology of his best work.

Lowe's philosophy that music should be fun and danceable is fully realised and Half A Boy is two minutes and fifty-two seconds of pure, unadulterated fun. Carrack again shows what a versatile musician he is with a superbly deranged Cajun Farfisa organ solo. The performances from the entire band make it a classic and it was rightly chosen as the album's lead single.

Since this was the MTV age this naturally necessitated a promo video which found Lowe and the band gamboling on a grotty-looking shale beach somewhere surrounded by scantily clad women. The single peaked at #53 in the UK but it deserved higher, at least as high as Dire Straits' Walk of Life which was cut from the same cloth as Half a Boy and peaked at #2 in the UK charts a year or so later.

After two greasy rockers, You'll Never Get Me Up in One of Those and the excellent Maureen, Lowe shifts gears with God's Gift to Women, a country rock song about a deluded tomcat that was full of Lowe's trademark trenchant humour.

After closing side one with the languid Gee and the Rick, and the bawdy (Hey Big Mouth) Stand Up and Say That, side two opens with the throwaway instrumental Awesome - which was becoming something of an unwelcome tradition on Lowe's albums. Although Lowe would say Awesome was his attempt to do a Fabulous Thunderbirds kind of track, (Lowe had produced the band's T-Bird Rhythm LP in 1982) the results are not particularly successful.

Fortunately the album perks up again with Breakaway which boasts some fine Everly Brothers harmonies and another fabulous organ solo from Carrack.

Love Like a Glove (co-written by wife Carlene and James Eller) is another highlight, given a bit of extra oomph by the guesting ex-Rockpile alumni Billy Bremner and the country segue continues with a straight read of Joe Allison's Live Fast Love Hard Die Young.

Although Lowe originally wrote the album's closer L.A.F.S. for Carrack, since Paul was still struggling to find a record deal at that time, Lowe decided to to record the song himself after being encouraged to do so by Elvis Costello.

"I wrote this song for [Paul] called Love at First Sight and we recorded it in a sort of Al Green Memphis groove, the sort of stuff he was doing in the early seventies. It worked pretty successfully... anyway Elvis heard it and he thought it was a great song, to my amazement - I thought it was a good record with Paul's singing but I didn't think it was a particularly good song. He said, "You ought to record it, and I said, "no, not for me." He said, "what if I produce it, if you fancy me having a go at producing it, and I'll put the kitchen sink into it.""

Costello was true to his word. In addition to commissioning a string arrangement by Robert Kirby, Costello brought along the TKO Horns (Jeff Blythe and Paul Speare on saxophones, Big Jim Paterson on trombone and Dave Plews on trumpet who had featured prominently on Elvis's 1983 album Punch The Clock) and turned it into a polished gem; slightly over-produced but a gem nevertheless.

As Costello had done on Tempted he wisely got Carrack in to duet and the results should have been enough to score a sizeable hit. Unfortunately the spotlight had swung so far away by Nick Lowe by this point that the single failed to score the hit its quality merited.

Cowboy Outfit is easily my favourite of the albums Carrack recorded with Nick Lowe during the first half of the 1980s and it was, rightly, warmly received by the critics upon its release.

"Mr. Lowe is back, in fighting trim," opined Robert Palmer in the New York Times. "His new album ... is his best collection of original songs and carefully selected obscurities by other writers. But the key is the Cowboy Outfit - that gives Mr. Lowe exactly the sort of rocking yet subtle, experienced yet spirited backup that he has needed since Rockpile's breakup in 1980. With Mr. Lowe on bass and the powerful and precise Bobby Irwin on drums, the Cowboy Outfit has a rhythm section that can push hard or lay back and swing. The pianist and organist Paul Carrack ... is a superb accompanist, sensitive to the stylistic demands of Mr. Lowe's exceptionally varied material. Martin Belmont ... knows when to pick lacy patterns, when to kick the band along with incisively rhythmic chording and when to let go and howl. Music this infectious could finally make Mr. Lowe a star in the United States. But even if it doesn't, the album and the tour should offer audiences, and Mr. Lowe, the chance to have a lot of fun."

Despite such bouquets the Cowboy Outfit album was greeted with almost universal indifference by the record buying public at large, limping to a meagre #113 on the Billboard Top 200 and failing to chart at all in the UK.

In mitigation for this injustice, the mid-eighties was the time of the big production - and 1984 was arguably its zenith. Lowe's low-fi approach was therefore simply out of step with public taste, which the Cowboy Outfit's leader acknowledged but offered no apologies for: "If you were in your mid-30s you'd had it, unlike jazz, for instance, or country-and-western. You couldn't be too old to be a blues singer. So I thought, well, I'll find a way to use the fact that I'm getting older, this thing that everyone tries to disguise and hide in the pop business. I'm going to shove it up front and use it as an advantage. The way I wanted to record myself, which I knew wasn't for everybody, I'd never get mainstream success, was for my records to have a certain under-produced, handmade quality to them."

****

The summer would prove to be cause for celebration for Paul Carrack when his beloved Sheffield Wednesday were promoted back to the top flight of English football after an absence of fourteen years. To commemorate this fact Carrack released a souvenir single entitled We Love You Wednesday. Although the single sank without trace it must have been nice for Paul to have a record out under his own name again.

Despite the decline in their commercial cachet Lowe and His Cowboy Outfit remained in demand as a live turn, as witnessed by their invitation to open for Bob Dylan at Wembley Stadium on 7th July 1984 and their support slot on Elvis Costello and the Attractions' North American tour throughout August and September.

Upon their return to the UK Lowe led his band back into the studio to record the Rose of England album which would eventually be released in August 1985.

Having started Cowboy Outfit with an organ driven tex mex ass-shaker Lowe repeats the trick with Darlin' Angel Eyes and the results are almost as successful.

The pleasant country rock She Don't Love Nobody (written by John Hiatt) is then followed by a blistering rockabilly cover of Seven Nights of Rock (originally recorded by Moon Mullican in 1957), which boasts a brilliant extended piano solo from Carrack sounding for all the world like Jerry Lee Lewis.

Long Walk Back (credited to the entire band, this was obviously something thrown together in the studio and played live) continues Lowe's frustrating tradition of including throwaway instrumentals on his records and can only be regarded as filler. What is more frustrating about such lazy knock-offs is the fact the album's title track that follows is one of Lowe's finest songs and reminded everyone what he could accomplish when he put his mind to it.

Although Lucky Dog (that follows the title track) was the sort of throwaway about which the critics always seemed keen to castigate Lowe it's hard to dislike and features some fine honky tonk piano work from Carrack.

After Lucky Dog comes the album's lead single - a remake of Lowe's pub rocker I Knew The Bride (When She Used To Rock And Roll). Although written by Lowe, it had originally been a hit for Dave Edmunds in 1977. A year later a live version by Nick Lowe's Last Chicken in the Shop was included on the Stiff Records compilation Live Stiffs Live.

For that reason there seemed little need to return to the song other than to perhaps reflect the fact Lowe was getting divorced from Carlene around this time.

Interestingly the updated version here was produced by Huey Lewis and featured his band, The News who were then one of the biggest acts in the world, unlikely as that sounds now.

Lewis and Lowe went way back when the latter had seen the former's band Clover in a Los Angeles club and convinced them to come over to Britain. However, Clover arrived in Blighty just as their pub-rock sound, was being replaced by punk rock. As a result the two Clover albums (produced by "Mutt" Lange) were not successful although the band - without Lewis - did back Elvis Costello on his 1977 debut album My Aim is True.

Despite the presence of Huey and The News (which did at least ensure the song got some attention and airplay) the remake was not especially successful, although it would become a minor hit on the Billboard charts.

Much better was Indoor Fireworks, on which Lowe publicly sums up the recent collapse of his marriage and lays bare his apparently broken heart. Written by Elvis Costello especially for his former producer Fireworks begins as a sparse ballad that quietly builds into a lush production number and was one of the album's saving graces.

The album then finishes with a couple of rather forgettable Lowe-penned country compositions, Hope to God I'm Right and the admittedly pretty I Can Be The One You Love and a couple of cover versions, Everyone (which boasts some delightful Everly Brothers harmonies from Paul Carrack on the chorus) and the silly and rather pointless Bo Bo Ska Diddle Daddle which was the sort of thing Lowe could knock off in his sleep and possibly did.

Containing as it does an instrumental cooked up in the studio and five cover versions (six if you include I Knew The Bride), Rose of England suggests Lowe was rather casually marking time until his muse returned, which, if one is being brutally unfair, wouldn't happen until his 1994 LP The Convincer.

In fact Lowe sounds enervated in places on Rose of England. It's still a professional and listenable album but a little of the twinkle and trademark

Lowe wit seems to have evaporated, and a lot of the tracks fade out as if Basher couldn't be bothered to come up with inventive ways of finishing his songs.

To be fair to Lowe, he has frequently acknowledged that he didn't always get it right on the records he made in the 1980s.

"I always wanted to do stuff with bottom," he admitted. "It's an old-fashioned expression and means something with substance, something with real feeling. But at that time, it didn't really come out right whenever I tried to do it. I was having too much fun or something like that."

Chapter Six

At the start of 1985 Carrack received an out of the blue invitation from Genesis's Mike Rutherford who was then seeking guest musicians for a solo project. Although Rutherford had tentatively named the new project Not Now Bernard, it would eventually see the light of day as Mike and the Mechanics.

With Genesis on hiatus while Phil Collins conquered the transatlantic pop charts, Rutherford had started writing songs in collaboration with B.A. Robertson and Hall and Oates producer Christopher Neil. The original plan had been to shop the fruits of their labours around in the hope that other artists might record them.

When that didn't happen Rutherford decided instead to record the songs himself and headed out to AIR Studios in Montserrat with keyboard player Adrian Lee and drummer Peter Van Hooke to lay down the backing tracks.

Rutherford had already released two solo albums: 1980's Smallcreep's Day (for which Carrack had been in the frame to sing lead vocals) and 1982's Acting Very Strange on which the Genesis guitarist had tackled the vocals, with mixed results. Although neither album had been warmly greeted by the critics, both had been moderately successful.

Deciding that tackling the vocals himself on his second album had been a mistake, upon his return to England, Rutherford decided to invite other singers to sing lead on the backing tracks he had recorded in Montserrat. Atop his wish list was Paul Carrack who had recently done a favour for Rutherford's co-writer.

"I bumped into B.A. Robertson who asked me to sing on a demo for him," Carrack later recalled, "he tracked me down. I had never met him but he tracked me down to sing on a demo of a song he had written and I did that, and he mentioned that he was writing with Mike for a solo album he was doing and would I be interested in coming down? So B.A. drove me down there [Fisher Lane Studios] one day."

The first track Carrack would tackle was Silent Running. Although most of the music had already been recorded in Montserrat, the song was still in embryonic form lyrically.

"There was this track," Carrack says, "a simple track but quite ethereal, they didn't have much of a lyric at the time just "can you hear me, can you hear me running," so I went in and sang. They liked what they heard. B.A. wrote this strange science fiction lyric so that was the first song I recorded with Mike and I really enjoyed because it was very different from what I was doing at the time."

The 'audition' passed, Carrack was invited to add his vocals to two more tracks.

Since Carrack was still swimming against the tide with Nick Lowe, he had grown interested in hearing how his voice might sound in a more polished eighties-style production setting, or, at the very least, a less resolutely low-tech setting.

"Music was becoming quite polished and poppy but Nick was really anti-all that, he was really old school," Carrack asserts. "That's why I was quite excited when I started with Mike and Mechanics because that was more of a contemporary set up and I quite fancied a crack at it."

Carrack, though, would not be the only singer lined up for the project. Feeling he also needed a strong rock singer to contrast with Carrack's soulful stylings, Rutherford had also invited former Sad Café frontman, Paul Young, to join the project.

Both Carrack and Young would later admit, their vocals completed, they thought no more about it and Carrack returned to the Cowboy Outfit to promote the Rose of England album.

Despite its failings, the critics surprisingly seemed inclined to give Lowe more of a break on Rose of England when it was released. The fact that most of the album was countrified and contained less of his usual genre-hopping seemed to help them at least pin Lowe down.

"So ends another long-playing chapter in the miraculous and obscure career of Nick Lowe," obliged Spin Magazine. "Another step closer to rock stardom or another brilliant and blind attempt in vain. As long as the charts are not the sole place a great musician is judged, Nick Lowe won't be all dressed up with nowhere to go."

Although the Cowboy Outfit was in the process of winding down, they would embark on one last US tour in the autumn.

As this review in Billboard magazine (which singled Carrack out for a special mention) makes clear, they remained an acclaimed live act to the last: "Rawness and directness remain the key qualities of Lowe's live repertoire. While he doesn't move around much himself, Lowe had a jammed Ritz crowd in a frenzy for most of the ninety-minute set. His Cowboy Outfit fits Lowe like a glove, thanks in large part to keyboardist / vocalist Paul Carrack. Barrelhouse rolls from the former Ace and Squeeze member added depth to Lowe's three minute hit mentality, as did Carrack's husky and evocative vocals.... Lowe and his group's unpretentious show is by far the best tension reliever in town. Lowe's tightly crafted pop performances provide an invigorating opportunity to let one's hair down and join the party."

At the conclusion of the Rose of England tour Lowe decided to dissolve the Cowboy Outfit. It seems that the decision was mutual and Lowe acknowledges that Carrack had been held back by his loyalty: "When we had our little group together he was really head and shoulders better than the rest of us but it was quite a rambunctious little outfit. We had a pretty good time or sort of a good time; there was a lot of boozing and what have you... He had a family the rest of us didn't and he looked around and said to himself this is going nowhere these guys are nice fellows but we're going nowhere, the records aren't very good and I need to do something about it. And he really took a conscious decision to change his act."

"Nick's low-tech approach to music was admirable in the face of the mid-eighties synthesiser pop boom," Carrack later remarked, "but after four years, several credible but low selling albums, numerous bus tours and a lot of laughs we called it a day."

Despite the low-key nature of the band's dissolution, Carrack association with Lowe had been a hectic and fecund period. Recording and touring virtually non-stop they had produced six and a half albums (four for Lowe, one for Carrack, one for Carlene Carter and a half for John Hiatt) that were filled with unquestionably great music that will endure longer than the trends that kept them off the radio and in the lower reaches of the charts. That's without even mentioning the countless thousands of concert-goers they'd entertained on both sides of the Atlantic and beyond.

Possibly because none of the records they made together set the world alight commercially, both Carrack and Lowe have both tended to downplay this period of their careers.

In Lowe's estimation the records he had made with Noise to Go and the Cowboy Outfit had been "rather patchy."

"I was churning out records when I didn't have enough good material," Lowe apologised in 1999. "I was seeking inspiration in a bottle…You can't do that consistently, though, and sooner or later, normally sooner, you get found out. I've always tried to do my best. But sometimes my best really hasn't been much good…I wasn't very good in the 1980s."

Lowe's assessment is excessively modest, in my view. The period might not have produced his finest ever records but Carrack and Lowe should nevertheless be fiercely proud of the work they did together.

****

As ever, Carrack (who would continue to act as Lowe's keyboard player on his next two studio albums - Pinker and Prouder Than Previous and Party of One) moved seamlessly on to his next project when in early October the eponymously titled Mike and the Mechanics album was finally released. Paul would sing three of the album's nine tracks - Silent Running (which opens the album), I Get the Feeling and A Call to Arms (which closes the album).

Although the lengthy and menacing synth intro gives one the initial impression that Silent Running was a Genesis outtake, once the song hits its stride it was clear it boasted a much punchier sound than one ordinarily associated with Collins, Rutherford and Banks. Even if you are not a fan of this sort of slick, overproduced, mid-eighties pop Silent Running is nevertheless a song that gets under your skin, secondly because its chorus is so infectious and primarily because it's got Paul Carrack singing the lead.

The song is notable, though, for having a much stranger lyric than one might expect of this genre - Carrack portrays a quasi-angelic shaman, on a mission to preserve society from being subsumed by some sort of distopian rule. Rutherford's presence is limited to two guitar solos and a few licks on the chorus, which complement the general effect of the song rather nicely. On the down side, the processed drums sound like someone tapping a crisp packet with a stick of rhubarb.

Although the synthetic keys and brass that envelop the breezy I Get The Feeling make it sound quite dated now, this was presumably precisely the sort of polished production setting that Carrack had "fancied a crack at." While Carrack takes to this new sound like a duck to water, perhaps he did so rather too well as this was the sound that would dominate his next solo album - One Good Reason - with not unconditional success.

Given the presence of Phil Collins and Tony Banks on the songwriting credits it will probably come as little surprise to learn that the atmospheric A Call To Arms originated from a Genesis recording session.

"It was a Genesis bit," Rutherford confirmed. "The main sequence had been discarded from [1983's Genesis album] and I always liked it, so I tried to do it and it didn't come out right. I had a couple of people play on it from a band I had produced and it's always a bad sign when you have to go through two or three singers!"

Rutherford received permission from his Genesis bandmates to use it for the Mechanics, then developed it into a full song with input from Neil and Robertson.

Bearing a lyrical similarity to Silent Running, the song (on which the Genesis influence remains prominent) focuses on a sudden uprising of the citizenry, compelled to fight against an unidentified foe. The lyrics are all tosh, of course, but the musicianship and the vocal interplay between Carrack, Young and backing singer Linda Taylor works very well.

Rutherford was delighted with the album: "The first album was fairly experimental. I had some songs, but it was very much week by week... My ambition was to have something outside Genesis that I could build on, rather than a casual project. I thought that if it did well, or at least got off the ground, I would continue it."

Given Rutherford's stature within the industry and the worldwide popularity of Genesis, Mike and the Mechanics was obviously going to garner sufficient attention on which Rutherford could build. What is perhaps surprising is just how well it did, particularly in America where initial reviews were far from promising.

"If you don't remember progressive rock," sniffed Chris Willman in the LA Times, "it's probably because most of its original practitioners don't, either. They're busy making pop albums like Mike & the Mechanics, which retains a little of the quasi-mystical sound of the old music but none of its ambition or vision. It's a comment not only on the changing nature of the genre, but on the changing purpose of solo albums, that Genesis guitarist Mike Rutherford has taken on a side project not to explore different territory but to make something as salable as possible. It seems to have worked... [Silent] Running works up more tension than the rest of the album, which is indistinguishable from the latest Alan Parsons Project and other like-minded efforts using lush electronic keyboard textures to over-inflate standard-brand love songs into something more significant-sounding. Even talented white-soul crooner Paul Carrack, undermined by such glitches as a what sounds like a cheap drum machine and a surprising lack of Rutherford's guitar, can't breathe much life into anything here."

Despite such negative reviews, what had started out as little more than a casual side project was soon gathering an increasing amount of momentum in terms of airplay and sales. Released as the first single off the album Silent Running did respectable business in the UK, climbing to #21 on the charts. In the US it did rather better, peaking at #6 (and also reached the top ten in Canada and Germany). As if to prove this was no fluke All I Need is a Miracle went one better, hitting #5 on the Billboard Hot 100. The third single off the album, the smooth adult oriented rock of Taken In, was also a hit in the US, reaching #32.

All of which must have been a tremendous source of pride for Rutherford given the amount of success his colleague Phil Collins was having around this time.

Rutherford, would later admit that he had been as surprised as anyone by the Mechanics' success: "One of the nicest moments in my career was when Atlantic chose the lead track Silent Running and it turned out to be a huge hit, yet nobody knew who did it. Suddenly, a musician quite far along in his career was able to put out new music and not be judged with any baggage."

With the album climbing to #26 on the Billboard album charts (it eventually sold over 500,000 copies in the US), and with its three singles having done so well a short North American tour of small venues was quickly organised in the summer of 1986, its brevity necessitated by Rutherford's commitments to Genesis.

Both singers signed on for the tour alongside Adrian Lee and Peter Van Hooke and, of course, Rutherford, supplemented by Paul Young's old Sad Café colleague, guitarist Ashley Mulford.

The 'Miracle Tour' kicked off in Miami on 5th June 1986 winding its way around North America until it came to an end on 9th July in Vancouver.

Since the Mike and the Mechanics album only had nine songs on it, the band was forced to look elsewhere for material to flesh out their repertoire. As it had been such a big radio hit in America Tempted was an obvious choice, while Rutherford also dipped into his own back catalogue, adding to the set list Half Way There, I Don't Wanna Know and Maxine (sung by Young) from Acting Very Strange and closing the show with a cover of the Spencer Davis Group classic Gimme Some Lovin'.

Despite the brevity of the sets, the shows were very well received. "Can Mike and the Mechanics keep an audience interested after playing their hits Silent Running and All I Need is a Miracle?" pondered Billboard Magazine. "If the group's world premiere performance here 5th June was any indication the answer is most certainly yes. The six-piece band, anchored by Genesis guitarist Mike Rutherford played a technically clean glitch-free show. Background vocals rang tight and in tune, solo turns were taken with confidence and tricky ensemble sections were negotiated without disruption."

A live recording from their gig in Philadelphia shows the band in fine fettle and the audience having a great time, with the two Pauls providing an interesting study in contrast. While Carrack, by his own admission, had always been a more sedate performer, Young proved to be a revelation as a showman and would become, in essence, the band's frontman.

"[Paul] was different person on stage," Carrack graciously acknowledged; "myself I'm kind of the same guy when I'm on stage but Paul he just came alive when he was on stage. He loved performing and he loved attention and he was a great singer and a great character."

"I think Mike has me in the band because I am a show off on stage and a bit of a rabble rouser," Young contemplated, "because even though they are all really good musicians and successful at whatever they do, without me they wouldn't have that kind of thing going. So they have me as the wild man and Paul Carrack is the straight singer, we play off each other and it does seem to work. I never thought it would, but it does."

Since the Mechanics project had exceeded all expectations it made sense to remain together and see what developed. Unfortunately the recording of and the promotional and touring duties for Genesis's Invisible Touch album would occupy Mike for the better part of the next two years.

****

In 1987 Paul signed a recording deal with Chrysalis Records. Although one might presume that this was on the back of his success with the Mechanics, this was only partially the reason. In actual fact, Paul had a lot for which to thank his old pal Huey Lewis who had acted as his cheerleader during a visit to London.

"I was mulling a record company offer at the time," Carrack reveals. "Then Huey went off to an awards dinner and spent the whole night bending the ear of his Chrysalis Records boss Chris Wright, telling him I was the greatest thing since sliced bread, and that if they didn't sign me they were crazy."

Sign him they did and with the Mechanics on hiatus the timing was perfect for Paul to record his third solo album.

As Carrack acknowledged, getting the opportunity to make another record had been a long and circuitous journey: "I went around with the same demo that everybody'd put in the trash bin before," Carrack said, "and all of a sudden everybody wanted to know again."

There was a catch. To ensure radio play for his first album, Chrysalis paired Carrack with Mike and the Mechanics producer Chris Neil. As a consequence the resulting album would sound a great deal more like a Chris Neil record than one by Paul Carrack.

To help make the album Neil roped in drummer Peter Van Hooke from the Mechanics, guitarist Tim Renwick and Paul 'Wix' Wickens who would go on to achieve wider fame as long-term keyboard player for Paul McCartney.

The presence of Wickens meant that Carrack wouldn't play a note on One Good Reason. "Chris (Neil) is the kind of guy who likes everything in place," Carrack explained, presumably hiding his indignation at this blow to his amour-propre. "You know, precise. I'm not precise."

The album kicks off with the title track One Good Reason. Although co-written with Chris Difford this was a long way from Tempted. If Carrack later came to regard Suburban Voodoo as frantic, that was nothing compared to this. Female backing singers, slapping basses and synthesisers abound with some screaming, spiralling lead guitars interjecting at every opportunity, so much so that Carrack sounds like a guest on his own song.

Much more tasteful was Carrack's cover of Jackie DeShannon's When You Walk in the Room (chosen because Chris Neil loved the song). Although Neil wisely eschewed a radical re-arrangement of what is, after all, a pop standard he did decide to present the song as a man and woman duet, casting Paul alongside former member of the English jazz-funk band Shakatak Jackie Rawe (with whom Carrack had worked whilst doing some session work for Graham Gouldman and Andrew Gold's Wax in 1985). Carrack and Rawe's vocals blend together very well it has to be said, making it an obvious candidate for a single.

The bouncy Hall and Oates-esque Button Off My Shirt was up next. Written by Billy Livsey and Graham Lyle this also was one of the better tracks on the album. Marinaded in a light island sauce with an effective, albeit brief, guitar solo from Renwick, Carrack's voice shines on this track lifting something essentially rather ordinary to levels beyond the reach of most of the people who were getting in the charts around this time. Despite the gamut of eighties production gimmicks (squawking female backing singers again feature large) Button off My Shirt is simply too catchy to dislike and was particularly impressive when Paul played it live. Carrack evidently also thought this was one of the more successful tracks on the album - including it on his 21 Good Reasons compilation in 1994.

Give Me a Chance was the first track solely penned by Carrack. Although the song doesn't break any ground lyrically the song proves to be a fine showcase for Carrack's wonderful voice. I would have preferred it with a less busy arrangement (the weedy synthetic soprano sax interpolations are particularly distracting) but even Neil's production style cannot botch what is a rather fine ballad (later covered by Tom Jones on his 1991 album Carrying a Torch).

Paul funks it up on the sprightly, danceable R & B-based Double it Up (co-written with Nick Lowe). This is in fact not a bad effort at a pulsating Motown crowd pleaser redolent perhaps of something Martha Reeves would have had a sizeable hit with in the golden age of Tamla. Once again, though, Neil's production succeeds in robbing the song of all spontaneity and, well, soul.

Okay, the album was an attempt to place Carrack squarely in the zeitgeist but a producer with a little bit of restraint or someone inclined to make Double it Up a more faithful homage to its influences could have given this song a much longer shelf life. As it was the song is redeemed by Carrack's vocals on which he again proves himself to be one of the world's greatest white soul singers.

Side two kicks off with the album's standout, the infectiously catchy Don't Shed a Tear. Written by Eddie Schwartz and Rob Friedman and brought to the sessions by Chris Neil the song was an obvious single and with its drive time feel and armourplated chorus it's easy to see why it went on to become such a massive hit in America.

The up-tempo Fire with Fire (written by Carrack and Neil) is next and although not one of the most memorable tracks of Paul's career it did allow him to let loose those amazing vocal cords and Wickens' organ solo is impressive. That said despite his hand in writing the song, I'm not convinced this is Carrack's bag at all. In fact the modern electronic textures employed here must surely have been privately anathema to him and again he seems like a stranger on his own song.

Much more satisfying is Here I Am, written by Huey Lewis and covered by Carrack as a thankyou for his pal's role in securing his record deal with Chrysalis. Employing an ersatz Jam and Lewis sound Neil's studio gimmicks seem very dated now (particularly the synth bass line). That said, this was the sort of thing that was being heavily rotated on American radio at the time, and judged on that standard, Here I Am works pretty successfully.

The darker Collrane (again written by Carrack and Neil) was the most Mike and the Mechanics number of the set and therefore seems rather atypical on One Good Reason. Essentially a mood piece based around one riff and a snatch of a bridge, the song sounds suspiciously like something cooked up in the studio. Despite such slight raw material Carrack really does prove that he could sing the telephone directory with an excellent vocal.

The album closes with a cover of (Do I Still Figure) In Your Life? (written by Pete Dello and made famous by Paul's fellow Crookes native, Joe Cocker). The least adorned song on the album allows Carrack's vocals room to shine and provides a blessed release after the big production numbers elsewhere. Although a bit of a chestnut Do I Still Figure was a lovely way to conclude the album: a sweet gesture of love from a man to his wife with some nice chord changes.

"We set out to make an album that would be played on the radio and would reach people. It's slightly more glossy, not quite as raw (as past solo work)," Carrack would assert once the album was in the can. "I have been very influenced by R&B music. As a teenager, that was what I was really into. I played in the local soul band; that was my first professional gig. Since then I've been through all kinds of changes. I'm thirty-six now, and I've been doing this since I finished school at sixteen. But R & B has always been there. I think that Motown and Stax stuff of the 1960s is the best music ever made."

****

Since One Good Reason would not be released until November 1987 this allowed Carrack to return to his non-stop workaholic ways when he accepted an invitation to join Roger Waters' backing band on a four-month tour in support of the former Pink Floyd leader's Radio K.A.O.S. concept album (on which Carrack had shared lead vocals on the track The Powers That Be) that had been released during the summer. (The album's concept was based around some of the big political issues of the day - the miner's strike, the effects of Thatcher and Reagan's monetarism, the bombing of Tripoli, the cold war - viewed through the eyes of Billy, a psychic but disabled twenty-three-year-old Welshman, who discusses his thoughts on these subjects in an on-air dialogue with Jim, a DJ at a fictitious local radio station, before eventually using his powers to simulate and then avert global nuclear destruction).

Dubbed the Roger Waters Bleeding Heart Band, Paul would take his place on keyboards and vocals alongside Graham Broad on drums, Doreen Chanter and Katie Kissoon on backing vocals, Mel Collins on saxophones, and Andy Fairweather-Low and Jay Stapley on guitars.

Paul admitted he just couldn't say no when someone offered him a well-paying gig: "There's a wife and three young mouths to feed at home. Besides, I like to keep busy. I really do enjoy my work."

For Waters the tour would be by far the largest and most ambitious of his solo career up to that point and was somewhat make or break. Having left Pink Floyd in 1985 assuming that would end the group, Waters had been surprised when his former colleagues David Gilmour and Nick Mason had elected to continue.

When the duo started working on a Pink Floyd record without him in 1986, Waters went to the High Court, arguing that without him the band was "a spent force creatively" and asking that his former colleagues be denied the right to use to the group's name.

Waters position seemed somewhat doomed to fail. Not only had Gilmour been the voice on virtually all of Floyd's best known songs, co-composer of some of the their best-loved works and his distinctive guitar style a major part of the band's appeal, he and Mason were the men in possession of the brand name and having invited back into the fold original keyboardist Richard Wright (whom Waters had fired in 1980), Gilmour knew three-quarters of the classic Floyd line-up would ultimately trump the claim made by their erstwhile lyricist, conceptual oarsman and bass player that the band should be dissolved. And so it would prove when, after a great deal of legal wrangling, Waters eventually ceded the rights to the group's name (in exchange for the ownership of The Wall).

To rub salt into Waters' wounds, while Floyd's first album without him would sell millions and top the international charts, and help to fill vast stadiums wherever they went (as opposed to the theatres that would accommodate Waters), Radio K.A.O.S. tanked, charting in just two countries, peaking at #25 in the United Kingdom and #50 in the United States.

To say that Waters was under pressure, then, is therefore something of an understatement, underscored by the fact that several of his tour dates would virtually coincide with Floyd playing in the same town.

"We were playing Toronto when Floyd were rehearsing just up the road," Carrack remembers. "Having them nearby added a bit of spice. There was tension there, and we all knew Roger was under a lot of pressure, but I think he felt vindicated because he was doing something different. We did some Floyd tunes, but not many."

Famously domineering and obstreperous at the best of times, Waters was the complete opposite of the laidback Nick Lowe or the gentlemanly Mike Rutherford and Paul, clearly in no mood to be treated as little more than a hired stooge, knew he had to assert himself.

"I know he can be intimidating and demanding," Carrack later explained, "but I wasn't having any of it, and I think he appreciated it. Roger's strength is the big concept. He really means it, and you can't fault his commitment, but he can make hard work of it. I think he sometimes finds it difficult to put over to the band what he wants, because basically his music is very simple and some of the musicians get a bit scared of what to play and how to play, because he doesn't always know how to put over what he's after."

As befitting his reputation as rock music's master of spectacle and pageantry the K.A.O.S. live show would be an elaborately-staged affair designed by Mark Fisher and Jonathan Park, who had worked with Waters on all of Pink Floyd's tours since 1977.

Presented as part of a live Radio K.A.O.S. radio special, with mock commercials, station idents and between-song banter from real-life California DJ Jim Ladd (reprising the role he had essayed on the album), the show also featured such props as quadrophonic sounds, circular screens (on to which animations and real footage of what the songs represented were screened) while a telephone booth positioned at the rear of auditoriums allowed the audience to direct questions at Waters.

Whilst recording Radio K.A.O.S. Waters had embraced new technology which essentially meant that his backing band would also have to, to enable them to recreate the album's songs. For Carrack this necessitated a crash course in the M1 Korg: "Radio K.A.O.S. got me into reading a few manuals, and getting over the fear factor. I found that I wasn't a complete blockhead as far as new equipment was concerend. Obviously, these instruments are made with musicians in mind."

Nevertheless, Carrack admitted that, "the first two or three shows were bloody nervewracking!"

"It was all synced to film," he elaborated. "There was some stuff on tape and we had all these headphones on stage with click tracks in 'em. I didn't play to them very much, though. I'd just get the cue, then take off the headphones and play with the drums. Fortunately, Roger liked what I did. He wanted heart. Once, though, I did get told off for over-soloing - getting a bit too flowery."

On several dates Paul would also act as the tour's unofficial support act, warming up the crowd usually with a solo version of Tempted (or, on one occasion, Say You Will from Suburban Voodoo).

The rest of set was culled from Waters' current album and his previous set The Pros and Cons of Hitchhiking and a selection of Pink Floyd favourites, two of which - Have a Cigar and Money - were sung by Carrack (who had also sang lead on the latter when it appeared on the b-side of the Waters single Sunset Strip).

Many fans, though, were not impressed by Waters decision to tamper with the sacrosanct Floyd classic.

"My version actually came out as a b-side, and I got death threats for it," Carrack chuckled. "They said I should be shot!"

This was not the only occasion Carrack was confronted by the extremes of Floyd's fanatical fanbase: "We saw rather a lot of madness on the KAOS tour. I can remember arriving at one gig and there was a guy outside who was convinced he was the character Billy from the album, and the whole thing had been written about him."

The tour started in Providence, Rhode Island North America on 14th August 1987 and ended on the 22nd November 1987 with two performances at Wembley Arena in London, England.

Though the two were very different people in temperament, Carrack said working with Waters had been surprisingly enjoyable: "I reckon if you were in a band with him for twenty years as an equal member, it would be a bloody nightmare, but that wasn't what this band was about. I think he had a certain respect for us, and we respected that it was his project, and we were trying to do our utmost to make it work for him. He's a very intelligent guy. He has a sense of humour, though it is black, but it's quite acute. He's no rock 'n' roll blockhead, you know ... like me."

****

With his obligations to Roger Waters completed Carrack could finally turn his attention to promoting One Good Reason which was released in November.

Prior to doing so Carrack announced that he was determined "to get this bloody solo thing happening."

"I enjoy being involved with other people's work," he stated, "and I've learned an awful lot from all the different people I've worked with. But now I think it's time that I should be putting some of that expertise to use for my own stuff.

"I've never really hankered after fame, and I don't care about stardom or anything like that. But, after banging my head against the wall for all these years, I'm really keen that this record should get on the radio and on the charts. I've always felt that a good artist gets better as he becomes older and more experienced, so I suppose that's now's as good a time for me as any."

Now certainly was as good a time as any. While he was completing his touring engagements with Roger Waters his album had been getting Stateside raves.

"Paul Carrack has certainly made the rounds," frothed Chris Heim of the Chicago Tribune. "He was a member of Ace and Squeeze and more recently provided vocal and keyboard support for ex-Pink Floyd member Roger Waters. But Carrack has always been at his best on his own, as his second solo album [sic] again proves. One Good Reason forsakes the cool, but decidedly less commercial pub-rock of his first album [sic] for more highly polished, keyboard-based modern dance rock. Carrack reworks a number of influences here - the Searchers and Joe Cocker, two of whose songs he covers; the Spinners, whose sound strongly influences several cuts; and the pop-rock style of Nick Lowe, and Chris Difford of Squeeze, who co-wrote two of the tracks. Carrack's change in direction may disappoint some, but this buoyant, breezy record offers not one, but many good reasons to stick with him anyway."

If Carrack was delighted with the reviews, the success of the album's first single was an even greater cause for celebration. After entering the Billboard Hot 100 chart at #72 in November 1987, Don't Shed a Tear (backed with Merrilee, Carrack's tribute to his recently newborn daughter) steadily climbed the charts until it peaked at #9 in February 1988, becoming Carrack's biggest U.S. hit as a solo artist. It eventually spent twenty-three weeks on the Hot 100, including thirteen weeks inside the top forty (strangely, it stalled at #60 in the UK charts).

With Don't Shed a Tear speeding up the Billboard charts Carrack hit the promotional trail hard and the press lapped it up.

"Critics have been raving for years that Paul Carrack is a polished gem," Jonathan Takiff staff writer with the Philadelphia Daily News bubbled on 26th February, "that he deserves the same degree of mass acceptance as fellow blue-eyed soulsters Phil Collins, Stevie Winwood and Daryl Hall. Carrack modestly suggests that his newly elevated status is "the culmination of many years of work, and of things falling into place for me.""

Encouraged by the success of Don't Shed a Tear and One Good Reason Carrack put together a band at short notice to undertake a short American mini tour of club dates.

As if already distancing himself from the unrepresentative sound of his album, tellingly none of the musicians who played on the album would join him on tour. Instead Paul would fashion the sound he wanted with the people he wanted. First on his list was Nick Lowe.

"Well, my idea of going on the road it that it's got to be fun," Carrack elaborated. "If I'm calling the shots, then I want guys who play with heart, who have the right attitude, so Nick was the first guy to be pencilled in. Plus, there was no way he was not going to come along, whether I wanted him or not."

The short notice meant Paul had to call in some favours from some of his other old friends and it says much for his popularity and standing within the industry that people were prepared to drop what they were doing to help him out. Alongside Lowe the band would be rounded out by Andy Fairweather-Low and Andy Newmark and keyboardist / additional guitarist Audie DeLone.

The tour got off to a flying start on 21st February at The Palace in Los Angeles where Don Waller from the LA Times was on hand to give the show a suitably fulsome review: "Backed by an Anglo-American quartet of pub-rock semi-legends and session heavies, veteran British keyboardist-vocalist Paul Carrack kicked off his first U.S. solo tour before a full house at the Palace on Friday with a raucous, rock-kissed soul number (Fire With Fire) that was about as good as such things get. A rather unprepossessing performer, Carrack is nevertheless a supple, soulful vocalist who's racked up five hits as the lead singer for four different acts over the last 14 years: How Long (Ace), Tempted (Squeeze), Silent Running (Mike & the Mechanics), I Need You (recorded under his own name) and his latest, biggest chartbuster Don't Shed a Tear (likewise). Carrack did 'em all, fleshing out the hour-plus set with the best half-dozen tunes from his current LP. Strong songs, strong voice, strong band--especially Andy Newmark. What more could you ask for? ... It might have been a band of lows - guitarist Andy Fairweather-Low was also aboard - but Carrack's show was mostly a night of highlights."

A few nights later Carrack was on the other side of the country performing at the Ritz in New York, a concert which was captured and screened by MTV.

Despite being among friends, Carrack endearingly seemed a tad diffident being in the spotlight. He need not have been uncomfortable as he was on tremendous form (despite complaining of laryngitis) and the audience clearly enjoyed themselves immensely.

In addition, the songs from One Good Reason worked so much better in a live setting than they had done when beaten into submission by Neil's production.

Mid-set Paul would generously hand the spotlight to Lowe who performed Half a Boy and Half a Man (replete with a particularly fuelled piano solo from Carrack) and I Knew the Bride When She Used to Rock and Roll.

With a top ten single, record company support and sell-out dates everywhere he went Carrack confessed to the Philadelphia Daily News that the current upturn in his fortunes had flabbergasted him: "For the first time in my life, every time the phone rings it's bloody good news, and that's bloody frightening."

However, just when it seemed things couldn't get any better Paul received news from home that his wife Kathy was seriously ill.

"We were on tour in the States," Carrack later recalled, "riding high with Don't Shed a Tear ... when I got the call [that] my wife was quite seriously ill, she'd been having problems for some time and we discovered that she in fact had a problem with her kidney and she needed major emergency surgery to take the kidney out basically, so I got the call about that and dropped everything and came straight home and at this time of course we had a very young family, also my wife had just given birth to our third child so that upset the apple cart a little bit but the main thing is that she is well and she recovered very well but at the time it was pretty tough."

Although Carrack was otherwise disposed dealing with a major family crisis Chrysalis Records promised to keep the fires burning and the label's executives were true to their word, releasing the follow-up singles One Good Reason which also managed to crack the US Top Thirty and When You Walk in the Room (which peaked at #90 in US and also crept into the UK top fifty).

While his biggest selling album to date (One Good Reason would eventually remain in the Billboard Hot 100 for almost half a year) and two top thirty US hits had demonstrated that Carrack could achieve commercial success under his own name, it had been at the cost of some identity, as Carrack acknowledged: "I did let Chris have a lot of influence on this album. I wanted it to be strong to get a good old foot in the door again. We made a posh-sounding album that's more accessible to a lot of people. But on the next one I intend to play a lot more, and I would want to put more of my personality in it."

"The only thing about the album I made, it was very poppy and very programmed and not quite as organic as I would have liked. People who liked what I did were a little put off by it, having said that it introduced me to other people who wouldn't have heard of me otherwise."

****

In April 1988, Mike reconvened the Mechanics to record the band's second album, Living Years. On this occasion Rutherford and his co-writers had the luxury of being able to write with his two singers in mind.

"I knew where I was going a little bit more," Rutherford acknowledged. "I mean, I was writing for the second time with Chris Neil and B.A. Robertson and those song writing relationships were developing and that happens… you work with people more and more and I think if the relationship is good, it gets better and the whole thing was easier because I knew who was singing; I could write it in the right key…"

Although the band's second album was written principally by Rutherford, Robertson and Neil, this time Paul Young also co-wrote a couple of tracks - Black and Blue and Beautiful Day. Strangely, there was not as yet a seat at the songwriting table for Carrack who also got the thin end of the wedge when it came to dividing up the lead vocal duties. While Young sang lead on six of the album's ten songs Carrack would be limited to just four - the stadium rocker Nobody Knows, the minimalist Don't, the Genesis-like Why Me? and The Living Years.

Even though it was abundantly clear that the album's standout was the latter song, the record company opted to release the Young-sung rocker Nobody's Perfect as the album's first single in October 1988.

For Carrack, Nobody's Perfect (which could only limp as far as #63 in the US charts) had seemed a peculiar choice: "I think to be perfectly honest with you, I'm not sure how the other chaps will think when they read this but I didn't really think Nobody's Perfect was a great first single although I think it is a good song and a great performance from Paul Young. I think the idea was they wanted a fairly upbeat first single before they came in with The Living Years. We always thought that The Living Years was going to be strong..."

Penned by Rutherford and Robertson The Living Years, was written to reflect the recent loss of their fathers in 1986, and the regrets that they shared that things had been left unsaid.

The weekend after they'd finished writing the song Rutherford and Robertson sat down to watch the televised coverage of Nelson Mandela's 70th Birthday Concert at Wembley Stadium (at which Carrack, incidentally, had performed How Long) during which they were moved and impressed by Eric Clapton's performance of Wonderful Tonight, a song written about his and George Harrison's ex wife Patti Boyd. "He sung it with such dignity," Rutherford swooned, "and you felt part of it without ever feeling uncomfortable. It seemed to me ... if Paul were able to impart the emotion with that same quality, then we would be okay."

They needn't have worried. As Carrack had lost his father, Ben, at a young age the lyrics held an extra poignancy, which was reflected in his stirring and emotive performance. Despite the universal appeal of the lyric it was Carrack's performance that provided that extra ingredient.

"B.A. and I were not sure when we were writing it whether it was going to work," Rutherford recounted, "it was a song about death in a way, if you got it wrong you would have failed but the writing was good and Paul sang it beautifully. I didn't realise at the time that Paul lost his father so young, he's quite reserved about things like that but I'm sure when he sang it it had feelings for him."

"The subject matter is about a difficult relationship with your father and regretting that more effort wasn't made in that respect," Paul would remark. "Now, I didn't have that problem myself with my own father he was a great guy and we all loved him the problem was I lost him too young so although I didn't relate entirely with the subject of the song I felt it I was able to give it that little bit of gravity that it needed and get a good performance out of it by understanding the loss element of it."

Alongside Tempted and How Long, The Living Years would become the song that people most commonly associate with Paul Carrack and, naturally, he continues to perform it to this day in his live sets.

"I'm very proud of my contribution to that," Carrack reflected. "I think it is a great song, it's a wonderful song but it could have turned out all wrong. I think it needed to have that empathy of someone who had experienced loss and I did experience the loss of my father as a young kid which had a profound effect on my whole life and my whole personality, so inasmuch as

I didn't really relate to the lyric of the song in the same way because I didn't have that difficult relationship with my dad I had a good relationship but I had that sense of loss which I'd always carried around with me for many years so maybe that had something to do with the fact that I was able to give a convincing performance to it..

"When I get to the verse I wasn't there that morning when my father passed away that's how I feel and I picture it in my head and I remember coming down the stairs and being given the news that my dad had passed away and it's a really heavy moment so now when I do that song live I always follow it up with something more light-hearted."

The song touched a nerve with practically everyone who heard it and skyrocketed to the top of both the UK and US charts, climbing to number two in the UK and going all the way to #1 in the Billboard Hot 100. The single's success also increased sales of its parent album, helping it climb to #13 on the Billboard chart.

With The Living Years proving to be even more popular than its predecessor, the band (augmented by Tim Renwick, now a highly respected session ace) would once again hit the road, this time starting in the UK and Europe.

Incredibly, promoters were initially wary of booking the Mechanics in the UK, as Mike explained: "The people wouldn't put us on because they thought we wouldn't sell any tickets. You know, if I'd said' "I want to play Birmingham" they'd have said, "fine, who to?" so then it happened and we booked a European tour with just Manchester, London and Folkestone… I don't know why Folkestone! That was all it was going to be at first and then when things took off we only had three days left at the end … as it is the tour finishes at Hammersmith and I'm off to America the next day! What was a five or six day gap is now… So, we've lost a few days off just to try and do a bit more in Europe…"

As the band was much more successful in the States, once again they proved a very popular live draw when the tour crossed the Atlantic, so popular in fact that extra dates had to be added to their schedule to satisfy demand in late summer.

During the tour the band somehow found the time to record a version The Beatles' Revolution for the soundtrack of American comedy duo, Cheech and Chong's latest movie, Rude Awakening.

"They wanted a song and I was in the studio," Rutherford recounted, "and I had no ideas at all and then we got this idea to do that track. There were several ways it could have come out and it ended up okay. We also did it as an encore at the shows in the States with the two Pauls duetting; one Paul sang the first verse; one Paul sang second verse and then on the third verse they both sang together but never the same words!"

At the end of the tour Rutherford decided it was time to take a break from the Mechanics. To be fair to him he had achieved all he had set out to do and more, establishing Mike and the Mechanics as a large act in its own right.

Asked to assess his work with The Mechanics at this point compared with some of the other groups he had worked with, Carrack replied, "It's different. It's a nice professional level and there is no corner cutting or anything like that, and it is fairly comfortable in that respect. A lot of the other things have been a lot more "improvised" [laughter] but musically you try to bring whatever you can and help in any way. When I first got involved with it in the 1980's whenever that was... at the time most of the projects I was involved with were very low tech. People like Squeeze and Nick Lowe... Nick wouldn't even have a synthesiser in the studio, he hated them, and so this was the opposite end of the spectrum, especially the first couple of albums which were dead posh sounding. To me it's all music and it is all valid, really."

Chapter Seven

To capitalise on the phenomenal success of The Living Years, Carrack was keen to begin work on his fourth solo album, Groove Approved. Initially, though, it was not a foregone conclusion that Chrysalis would allow him to proceed.

The sticking point appeared to be that Carrack no longer wished to be produced by Chris Neil.

"Chris doesn't see the beauty in anything that's kind of 'dodgy,'" Carrack cavilled, "I'm not a perfect kind of person, I'm a bit dodgy. So for the record to be me, it has to have some spontaneity, and that's what the first album was missing."

In a bid to move away from Neil's "clinical approach" Carrack decided he would co-produce the new record himself alongside another former Hall and Oates producer - Tom 'T-Bone' Wolk - who became involved at the suggestion of Carrack's manager, Jake Riviera.

Recalling his first meeting with Carrack, Wolk was impressed with how down to earth his new collaborator was: "Paul picked me up at the bed and breakfast where I was staying, he said, "Hi, I'm Paul." I said, "I'm T-Bone." He said, "I guess we should write some songs." We hit it off immediately."

Although the first fruits of their collaboration - Only My Heart Can Tell and Loveless - were both strong, Chrysalis still seemed reluctant to green light an album.

"All that remained," Carrack sighed, "was to convince the record company that we weren't a couple of jerks, that we knew what we were doing, and that wasn't easy, believe me."

Fortunately, after working up a few tracks on a trial basis, Chrysalis eventually gave the go-ahead.

As Carrack was due to complete the second leg of the Mechanics' American tour, it made sense to make a start on the album while he was Stateside, specifically at The Hit Factory in New York, where he could call upon some stellar names such as Michael McDonald (with whom he would co-write Love Can Break Your Heart) and Daryl Hall (who contributes backing vocals to Love Can Break Your Heart and I'm on Your Tail). With Wolk on bass and guitars the rest of Groove Approved's supporting cast would be filled out by drummer Jimmy Bralower, Pretenders / Paul McCartney guitarist Robbie McIntosh and, on organ and keyboards, a certain Paul Carrack.

Having been been upset by Neil's decision to ignore his instrumental prowess on One Good Reason Carrack was delighted that Wolk wanted to utilise it.

"I was overwhelmed by what an outstanding rock and roll and R&B keyboard player he was," Wolk affirmed, "and I felt that people needed to hear that on this record."

"It's a bit raggedy and I like that," Carrack asserted. "I didn't play a note on the previous album. Chris [Neil] is the kind of guy who likes everything in place. You know, precise. I'm not precise. T-Bone loves the way I play."

By writing or co-writing all ten tracks on the album Carrack was also making it plain that he didn't wish to be pushed into songs that he didn't wholeheartedly like, as he had on One Good Reason.

The album begins with the Carrack and Wolk co-write Only My Heart Can Tell and it's apparent that Carrack's sound had evolved from his previous record. The sound is more organic, literally - Paul's Hammond happily returning to replace the synth heavy palette of before.

However, if Only My Heart Can Tell marked a departure from One Good Reason's sound I Live By The Groove is rather a return to it.

Having scored such a big hit with Don't Shed a Tear it was only natural that Carrack should want to return to its source to see if he could repeat the formula. Teaming up with Tear's co-writer Eddie Schwarz (who also co-produced this track), the result was another bespoke pop soul groove and although it was chosen as the album's lead single it couldn't repeat the success of its predecessor.

An early album highlight, though, is I Live on a Battlefield - written by Nick Lowe. According to Carrack, "Battlefield was originally a very "skiffle-type demo," that clearly needed a bit of tweaking. Taking Lowe's raw materials Carrack fashioned the song into an unabashed Motown homage (and earned a co-writer's credit); one that was so authentic that one could easily imagine The Supremes having had a hit with it. Miss Diana Ross evidently agreed, covering the song on her The Force Behind the Power album.

"For me Nick Lowe is one of England's most underrated songwriters," Carrack rhapsodised. "I was honoured to contribute in a small way to this brilliant composition. The song was later covered by Diana Ross after we were asked by her producer to write a middle bit."

Next up was the smoothly soulful Love Can Break Your Heart, which Paul co-wrote with blue-eyed soul avatar Michael McDonald whose distinctive backing vocals ring out strongly on the chorus.

Carrack later revealed that his partnership with the former Doobie Brother (who recorded his own version of Love Can Break Your Heart on his 1990 LP, Take it to Heart) came about after several unsuccessful play dates set up by Chrysalis aimed at getting him to write with some totally inappropriate industry hacks.

"I was in L.A.," Carrack shuddered, "and my record company was pitching me songs and pitching me songs and saying, "We think you should get together with other writers." I had only written with people like Nick (Lowe) so they set up a bunch of meetings for me to meet the old LA tunesmiths.

I'm not knocking these guys, some of them had good reputations, but it was very, very weird. This one guy, bold as brass, was sitting by the swimming pool in his hotel, and he's got a ghetto blaster. He puts on the old backing track and gives me a whole performance by the swimming pool."

The second co-write with Nick Lowe on the album was I'm On Your Tail. With faux audience whoops throughout Carrack and Wolk were clearly intent on creating the illusion that the song was recorded live in some smoke-filled underground New York jazz club. Whilst compositionally and lyrically slight Carrack raises it above the merely generic with an energetic performance and its looseness recalls the appeal of Suburban Voodoo.

Self-confessedly more comfortable writing with his mates, Carrack collaborated with Chris Difford on After the Love is Gone. Strangely given that it was written by two former Squeeze colleagues the song sounds a lot like Hall and Oates, although that of course is no bad thing.

Loveless, meanwhile, is a lovely soul ballad, delivered with real panache by Paul. Listening to the track nowadays it seems to me that plenty of artists had hits with this sort of thing in the 1990s and it was such an obvious album highlight that it deserved a much wider audience. Instead, although Chrysalis went to the trouble of remixing it in preparation for its release as a seven-inch (Joe Mardin adding a string arrangement) the single was ultimately shelved.

While Tip of My Tongue (which featured fellow Mechanic Paul Young on backing vocals) was another track custom built for adult-contemporary radio stations, Dedicated is one of Carrack's best heart-on-sleeve ballads, and another one of the album's undoubted standouts with some gorgeous chord changes and an appropriately unblemished vocal.

In the hands of someone like Whitney Houston Dedicated would have been a monster hit. It wouldn't have been as good, but it would have been a big hit and the sort of thing that crops up as a first dance at weddings. Again it's criminal that this wasn't a big hit in any of the larger markets although it did reach the top twenty of the Dutch charts.

Having doffed his hat to his soul and R&B influences elsewhere on the album, Groove Approved concludes with a clear homage to another inspiration, Van Morrison, on Bad News at the Best of Times. With its mandolin and accordian accompaniment this seemed a little out of step with the rest of the album, although again that's no bad thing, showing Carrack's versatility to great effect.

Perhaps it's worth suggesting that if Van the Man had written this it would have had the critics drooling, Radio Two producers rotating it, fellow artists seeking to cover it and buskers rushing to learn it. Instead, regrettably, it remains a largely obscure Paul Carrack album track.

Released in September 1989, Groove Approved, although something of a curate's egg, did mark a significant improvement on One Good Reason if only for the decision to eviscerate Chris Neil's obtrusive production sheen. Certainly Paul was satisfied with the results: "One Good Reason was a good record, but it wasn't completely my record. I wanted Groove Approved to sound more like me, and I wanted it to make a bit more of a personal statement. I think we've succeeded at that.

"I think this is the best record I've done. I've been doing this long enough that I could probably make any record you could ask me to make, but this is the kind of record that I like best and kind of record I think I should be making."

Carrack couldn't get over how ironic was that it was only now, after two decades in the business he had finally been given the chance to forge a record that he felt best represented how he wanted to sound.

"To most people I'm a new artist," he asserted. "For myself as a musician, I still feel I'm only just scraping the tip of the iceberg in a lot of ways. Maybe I'm just a slow learner. I'm thirty-eight. I've been drifting around, doing this and that. Thirty-eight, when most people are finished in this game and I'm only getting to make what feels like my first bloody record. It's weird, eh?"

Sensing that the wind was changing at his record company, however, Carrack seemed unsure whether the album and its spin-off singles would be hits: "I don't know if we'll be building a mansion or anything from this record, but my wife is expecting a fourth child in February, and I'm hoping it does well enough at least for me to extend into the loft."

In the event, without a single as bulletproof as Don't Shed A Tear (or, that is to say, without a record company who could recognise that it had one in Loveless) or a similarly generous promotional budget the album was markedly less successful than One Good Reason - although this was almost certainly more to do with the unsettled situation at Chrysalis which was in the process of being sold to EMI during this period (50% of Chrysalis Records was sold in 1990, the remaining half in 1991, with both its catalogue and artists, Carrack included, being shifted to the main EMI imprints).

While One Good Reason had introduced Carrack as a bona fide solo act, the comparative failure of Groove Approved checked his momentum and it would be another six years before he would release another solo record.

Fortunately there was a boost for Carrack when Linda Ronstadt included two Carrack songs - I Need You and So Right, So Wrong - on her Cry Like a Rainstorm, Howl Like the Wind album, released in October 1989.

"Danny Ferrington, my roommate - and a wonderful guitar maker - loves Paul Carrack's songs," Ronstadt explained. "He just kept bugging me about him for such a long time that I finally took his word for it. I Need You was a song I'd suggested for Smokey Robinson because he wanted to do a duet with me, but he just didn't hear it. So I kept it on hold because I knew it would be a great duet some day."

With Smokey unavailable Ronstadt turned instead to Aaron Neville to duet on I Need You and the results must have pleased Carrack no end, particularly since Cry Like a Rainstorm, Howl Like the Wind went on to become one of the American sonstrel's best-selling albums, shifting over three million copies in the United States alone.

****

In 1990 Carrack returned to the Mechanics fold. With Phil Collins still touring in support of his ...But Seriously LP this gave Mike Rutherford the opportunity to begin writing the songs that would become the Mechanics' third album, Word of Mouth.

Although Rutherford would again carry out the bulk of the writing work with Chris Neil and B.A. Robertson, this time he would also invite Carrack to participate in the writing process.

On 22nd February 1990, Carrack and the rest of the Mechanics attended the 32nd Grammy Awards. The Living Years was nominated in three categories: Record of the Year, Best Pop Vocal Performance by a Duo or Group and Best Music Video, Short Form. Although they missed out on a gong (losing out to Bette Midler's Wind Beneath My Wings, Linda Ronstadt & Aaron Neville's Don't Know Much and Michael Jackson's Leave Me Alone respectively) they were given the honour of performing the song live during the ceremony, backed by a boy's choir and a gospel choir. Although Paul would describe this as a career highlight he would also admit it was one of the most nerve-wracking experiences of his life.

"On the front row was Ella Fitzgerald, Ray Charles, Michael McDonald and Stevie Wonder," Paul later trembled, "it was absolutely terrifying."

Carrack needn't have worried, delivering as he does a faultless and powerful performance, which rightly earned him and the band a standing ovation.

Since the Mechanics were not due to start work on Word of Mouth until later in the year Carrack was afforded a rare opportunity to re-activate his dormant second career as a session musician, playing organ on Bob Geldof's Vegetarians of Love album and keyboards on Aztec Camera's Stray.

Thanks to all the success he'd enjoyed as a solo act and as a Mechanic he found he was now receiving fewer offers to work with other people: "It seems that when you do get a successful solo thing going, people assume you don't want to do them because you're too busy with your own career."

Almost certainly the most exciting sideline for carrack during 1990 would occur on 21st July when he was belatedly asked to take part in Roger Waters' lavish re-staging of Pink Floyd's rock opera The Wall in Berlin (to commemorate the fall of the Berlin Wall eight months earlier).

"Roger gave me this twenty-minute spiel about how it was going to be the biggest concert of all time, and so on," Paul recalls, "Finally, he came to the point and asked me: did I have Huey Lewis's phone number. I did and I gave it to him, then asked, "What about me Roger?" and he just said, "You're not famous enough!" There was no attempt to spare my feelings. In fact, Roger probably took great delight in telling me that. I thought it was perfectly reasonable, though. Nobody did know who the bloody hell I was."

However when Huey Lewis cried off Waters was forced to go back to the previously snubbed Carrack: "A week before the gig, Roger rang me up again. They were already over there rehearsing, and I think they were having one or two problems with the special guests. Roger said, "I want you to listen to these six songs and learn them, just in case." And then, two days before it all kicked off I got the call to go over."

The historic event was staged on the empty area between Potsdamer Platz and the Brandenburg Gate and attracted a sell-out crowd of over 350,000 people (which broke records for a paid-entry concert).

Designed by Mark Fisher and Jonathan Park, the stage featured a 550-foot-long and 82-foot-high Styrofoam wall and more special effects than a Hollywood blockbuster. Most of the wall was built before the show and the rest was built progressively throughout the first part of the show. The wall was then symbolically knocked down at the end of the show.

Carrack, who admitted he had been uncharacteristically nervous prior to his performance, would appear at the start of the second act to sing Hey, You, obscured by the partially built wall.

"Had I known I'd have offered to wear a paper bag over my head," he joked. "It was very scary, it really was the biggest gig of all time. If the cameras had seen me, they'd have caught my knees knocking."

Although Carrack had reportedly done so many interviews prior to the gig that he blew his voice out during the performance, he would nevertheless describe the concert as one of his, "proudest moments on stage."

The concert garnered gushing reviews, including several that singled Carrack out for special kudos.

"Waters," praised People Magazine, "wisely recruited some of the very best rock singers to perform it with him. Bryan Adams, for example, pumps new energy into a rugged rendition of Young Lust, while Paul Carrack, who joined the show at the last minute, belts out Hey, You with a passion that surpasses the original."

Not that Carrack let this success go to his head. "I think the following week," he would later remark, "I was playing in the Half Moon in Putney with Nick Lowe!"

***

In late 1990, Rutherford reconvened the Mechanics to begin work on Word Of Mouth. The initial plan had been to record in September but sessions had to be postponed when Carrack was laid low by a sinus infection. Although Carrack, ever the trouper, offered to play through the pain, Rutherford instead opted to delay proceedings until he had fully recovered.

This inauspicious start would set the tone for the rest of Word of Mouth's sessions. By all accounts the album was not a happy one to make.

Hanging over the album's recording sessions was not only a pressure to repeat the success of The Living Years but also a dreadful timing issue. Rutherford was shortly due to return to Genesis to record the sequel to their Invisible Touch behemoth. Although this did not necessarily mean that Rutherford was keeping his best ideas for his day job, it did mean that time was tight (made tighter by the delays caused by Carrack's illness).

In addition, since it was abundantly clear that they would not be able to tour in support of the album due to Rutherford's prior commitments this was a source of unrest within the Mechanics' ranks.

To complicate matters further Mike had decided to bring in a new producer - Russ Titelman - who had worked with George Harrison, Brian Wilson, Stevie Winwood and Eric Clapton among others. It was a decision that it seems the head Mechanic almost immediately regretted: "I decided to make a change in the choice of producer. Russ was originally producing it and I like his work very much but it just didn't seem to work and on the second day I said to everyone in the band 'I don't think this is going to work' and they all said; 'oh, give it a try…' Sometimes things would go great but after about two and a half months, I wasn't enjoying it and found myself driving to work very slowly!"

Titelman eventually stuck around for four months before Rutherford finally summoned the courage to politely inform him that his contributions were not what he was looking for.

As the pressure increased on Mike to return to Genesis, he eventually brought Chris Neil back into the producer's chair to see the half-finished album through to completion.

"Then Chris Neil came back and we weeded out some songs and by then the whole thing had become a bit of a problem," Rutherford declared. "I'd lost interest and it was laboured. I'm sure that was reflected on the album, but having said that; some stuff was very good. Get Up I like very much, and

89

Word Of Mouth as well… There's a bit more drive to it and The Mechanics are more about moods and atmospheres and somehow I think that was missing from this album…"

Having replaced the "moods and atmospheres" with real musicians (augmented on this album by touring mainstay Tim Renwick) Word of Mouth actually sounds like the work of a band and, in my own view, is much the better for it.

The tone is set right from the opening track, the danceable Get Up, co-written by Carrack and Rutherford which the latter described as "Van Halen meets Bruce Hornsby." Admittedly the piano part is very redolent of Hornsby's busy melodic style and Rutherford does contribute a strangled guitar solo but this wouldn't have sounded out of place on a Carrack solo album, which is maybe why I like it so much.

Strangely, although the song was pressed as the album's third single, it was withdrawn from stores and replaced by Stop Baby for reasons which remain unexplained and irrational, primarily because Rutherford had singled out Get Up as one of his favourites on the record and secondly because it clearly had such commercial potential.

Carrack's second vocal on the album was A Time and Place which sounds like it could close the credits of a heart-warming Disney animation, possibly involving talking animals. That said, A Time and a Place remains a nice ballad that Carrack sings with tremendous sincerity.

Carrack's second co-write on the album, meanwhile is The Way You Look at Me, which was a very strong piece of pop soul, with a particularly effective chorus. Both its writers were reportedly pleased with this track and it might have made a good single had it not clocked in at almost five minutes long.

Although written by B.A. Robertson and Mike Rutherford, the latter would acknowledge that Carrack was largely responsible for the final arrangement of Everybody Gets A Second Chance: "It was one of those songs, we had two cracks at it. I had a different version. You have an idea in your head on how a song's going to be and we put it down my way and it wasn't working and then Paul Carrack who actually came in one day and fiddled about on the keyboard and tried it much more in the style of the old Tamla Motown sort of swing vein and suddenly it came to life. It's one of those moments in the recording studio where you get a bit of luck…"

Carrack was next up on My Crime of Passion (which he co-wrote with Rutherford and Adrian Lee), a song about losing love which jars with the song's rather shiny happy accompaniment. That said, My Crime of Passion was a good composition which rather underlined what the Mechanics had been missing by waiting until their third album before allowing Carrack some substantial creative input.

The album closes on the more atmospheric lament to lost love Before (The Next Heartache Falls). Co-written by Rutherford and Carrack the song was clearly intended as the album's big centre-piece (clocking in at 6:38). After a slow burn the song kicks into life around the two-and-a-half-minute mark with the arrival of its big drums, guitar solos and all the other stadium rock accoutrements.

If there had been a video for the album's closer you could easily imagine Rutherford miming the solo on the precipice of a windswept mountainside wearing a billowing overcoat. While these sort of songs had tended to be the province of Paul Young within the Mechanics Carrack shows he had a strong rock voice when required.

While Rutherford bemoaned the lack of moods and atmospheres on Word of Mouth I think the record benefits by the move towards a more organic, muscular and human pop sound and the result is a highly listenable album.

Although the Mechanics' third album received decidedly mixed reviews in the UK, Vox magazine's reviewer was at least pleased that Carrack was doing well: "Well, I'm glad that after years before the mast with Squeeze and Nick Lowe, Paul Carrack has finally found fame with Mike and the Mechanics. Not that the band will ever be anything other than a hobby for guitarist Mike Rutherford; his day job is Genesis, and when they lumber around their inevitable summer stadium tour, they'll no doubt find room for a medley of Mike's greatest hits. A competent and appealing album for those who are fed up waiting five years for a Genesis album."

Word Of Mouth was eventually released on 25th March 1991, preceded by the rousing title track (sung by Young) which was issued as the first single on 4th March.

Whereas in the past Mechanics releases had performed better in the US charts than at home, Word of Mouth would see a complete reversal of fortunes. While the album and lead single could only scrape to #107 and #78 in their respective Stateside charts both strolled confidently into the top twenty in the UK. Likewise, although the second and third singles off the album (Everybody Gets a Second Chance and Stop Baby) failed to chart in the US both crept inside the top sixty in the UK.

Although this was not a bad showing, given the absence of a tour and a fairly desultory promotional campaign, there was a sense that this album deserved better.

Times, though, had changed drastically since The Living Years, particularly in the United States. While the years 1988 and 1989 had also seen #1 hits by such Heritage Rockers as The Beach Boys (Kokomo), Phil Collins (Groovy Kind of Love, Two Hearts and Another Day in Paradise), George Harrison (Got My Mind Set On You) and Stevie Winwood (Roll With It), by 1991, with the advent of rap, grunge and a whole variety of other confections, those days were gone in the U.S., never to return. In fact Mike and the Mechanics would never have another Stateside hit record.

Chapter Eight

With his solo career somewhat in abeyance thanks to the upheavals at his record company and the Mechanics on hiatus following Rutherford's return to Genesis, Carrack was available to accept an invitation to join Spin 1ne 2wo - a supergroup apparently dreamt up by an executive at Sony Music in Italy and assembled by widely respected session guitarist Phil Palmer (nephew of Kinks Ray and Dave Davies). The idea was to form a band filled with the best names in the business on their respected instruments and evidently bash out a one-off album of iconic rock covers.

Joining (or rather backing) Carrack on this brief collaboration would be drummer Steve Ferrone (ex-Average White Band), producer and keyboard player Rupert Hine and bass guitarist and Chapman stick poster boy Tony Levin (Peter Gabriel, King Crimson) and the aforementioned Palmer.

The songs chosen for the project were an interesting and eclectic mixture that comprised Bob Dylan's All Along the Watchtower, Led Zeppelin's Kashmir and a largely instrumental Black Dog, a soul-infused stab at Cream's White Room, The Who's Who Are You, Bad Company's Feel Like Making Love, Canned Heat's On The Road Again, Jimi Hendrix's Angel, Steely Dan's Reelin' In The Years, Blind Faith's Can't Find My Way Home, Tim Hardin's Reason To Believe and The Supremes' You Keep Me Hanging On.

Having chosen such a well-known set of classics, the musicians treated each with a tremendous amount of respect, perhaps too much as, with only one or two exceptions (the slowed down You Keep Me Hanging On, for example) the readings are fairly straightforward. Nonetheless the love of the songs shines through in the performances and everyone concerned is audibly having a great old time. Carrack, in particular tackles his vocal and Hammond organ duties with tremendous gusto and it must have been terrific fun for him to sink his teeth into this side of the rock and roll spectrum - after all, it wasn't the sort of thing for which he was especially renowned.

With so many in-demand session men involved and therefore highly likely to be off doing their own thing at a moment's notice Spin 1ne 2wo was never ever going to be a workable long-term project and so it would prove.

"[It was a] nice idea, and we had fun," Tony Levin would remark, "but as usual with projects of this kind, everyone's schedule didn't allow for much touring together. Projects are always limited unless the whole band can make that ensemble its main priority - then you become a band."

A pleasant diversion therefore is what it remained and when it was over Carrack was on to his next project which, surprisingly, turned out to be a return to Squeeze.

****

Times had changed for the band since Carrack had last worked with them over ten years previously. After surprisingly splitting up the band in 1982 (which Tilbrook would later describe as having been, "a knee-jerk reaction to doing too many tours back-to-back with too many albums, too many changes of keyboard players, too many changes of managers; the whole thing had steamed out of all proportion"), the band's songwriters had remained a team to record one album as a duo. When that proved only moderately successful the pair reconvened the band in 1985 with drummer Gilson Lavis, a returning Jools Holland and new bass player Keith Wilkinson. Although this version of the band stayed together to record Cosi Fan Tutti, Babylon and On (which featured the hit single Hourglass), Frank and the live album A Round and a Bout, Holland then left for a second time and he was replaced in the studio for their ninth album, Play, by Steve Nieve.

1992 though had been a year of upheaval for the group. After being dropped by A&M, Play had been released on Warner Brothers / Reprise but due to disappointing sales that would remain their only record for the label, and Squeeze returned to their A&M home.

Around this time drummer Gilson Lavis had also departed acrimoniously and shortly afterwards Difford finally decided to seek help for the alcoholism that had been threatening not only to derail the group but also to kill him. The fact that he made the decision to inform his bandmates that he was going into rehab literally just minutes before they were due to get on a plane bound for a six-week tour of North America had left Tilbrook as the only remaining founding member of Squeeze left in the band (Tilbrook continued the tour alongside Wilkinson, Nieve and Pete Thomas). At this stage the band looked finished.

Fortunately twelve weeks in rehab revitalised Difford and when his course of therapy was over he was a new man determined to piece his life back together and make a truly great record with Squeeze.

Towards the end of 1992 Difford was well enough to return to live work, taking a full and active part in Squeeze's acoustic shows for which Carrack had agreed to act as the opening act, and it was from there that the idea took root for their former keyboard player to return to the band full time.

"He just happened to be in town, in London, when we were doing an acoustic show," Difford elucidated. "We thought it was a bit of a long shot, but we asked him to open for us and he did. The next thing we knew, we were rehearsing for the album, and I put the motion forward that we should use Paul. So we put it to the test, and [it] worked out marvelously."

Paul, however, was not making any promises about making his return to Squeeze an indefinite stay: "We're just sort of playing it by ear and taking it as it comes. I'm really enjoying playing with the band, but I think everyone understands that I'm feeling the need to get my solo thing going again. The last time around it got a bit frustrating, because at the time being in Squeeze was a twelve-months-a-year commitment, but now it's a lot less pressurised. And because I've got other outlets now, with Squeeze I can sit back and enjoy playing keyboards and singing the occasional song. I've always been a fan of the band and of Chris and Glenn's songwriting, and I think the unit we've got now - musically and personally - is really great."

The band - Difford, Tilbrook, Wilkinson, Thomas and Carrack - set to work on what would become the Some Fantastic Place album at Glenn Tilbrook's newly-built home studio in Blackheath.

Having written together mano a mano (something they had rarely done before - a move they would claim revitalised their songwriting partnership and their friendship), Difford and Tilbrook also decided that the album would be an album of songs rather studio constructions.

"Before we started the album," Tilbrook declared, "we sat down and decided that we should strip away everything that's not absolutely necessary, anything that made the songs less direct. So in the writing and the arranging and the recording, there was this constant process of pairing the songs down, which I think has made it a better album and an album that will stand a better chance in the marketplace."

Although virtually the entire album would, as usual, be written by Difford and Tilbrook (the exception being the tropical-flavored True Colours - contributed and sung by Keith Wilkinson), all the band members new and old would contribute their creative voices to the making of the album.

"There was more open debate on the album than there's been on any other Squeeze record, and I think that's helped to make it one of our better ones," Difford confirmed. "There was a lot of to-ing and fro-ing on the arrangements. Everybody had very fierce ideas of the way the songs should be, and everybody stood firm on what they thought was right. That was great, because it showed that people really cared."

It's difficult to over-emphasise what a cracker Some Fantastic Place is. It's an album packed with invention, fun, confidence, great playing, great lyrics and great singing (mostly by Tilbrook, with the increasingly mic-shy Difford relegated to background harmonies, somewhat low in the mix). Above all it was a mature, cohesive album without a duffer in sight and, put simply, if you like pop music, you'll love this album.

The title track was an exceptionally fine piece of work, recorded as a moving tribute to Maxine Barker (an early girlfriend of Tilbrook's who had died of leukemia in 1992), and would be regarded by Difford as the finest song he and his partner had ever written. Fittingly everyone plays a blinder on the song with Carrack in particular contributing a wondrous organ part and some particularly beautiful backing vocals.

But the title track was just one highlight of many: from the organ-driven Everything in the World to the classic pop of It's Over and Talk to Him (both of which boast more twists and turns than a Raymond Chandler thriller), from the typically quirky but compelling Cold Shoulder (in which the song's protagonist gets his head stuck in a catflap after a lover's tiff) to the spry rockabilly of Third Rail and the elegant and blackly humorous Jolly Comes Home, and from the psych-tinged rocker Images of Loving to the album's closer, the McCartney-esque Pinocchio, the album was overflowing with winners.

For many of Squeeze's unshakeably loyal fans Some Fantastic Place would be a career peak, a view shared by Difford and Tilbrook.

"I always look back on this record and that particular year as being the pinnacle of my writing career," Difford stated proudly. "I had this black cloud over me that had gone and I was open to communication. I really enjoyed being around Glenn and this fantastic new band we had."

As with East Side Story it made sense to allow Paul at least one lead vocal on the album and the smoochy, smoothly-soulful Loving You Tonight would prove to be another winner, with Carrack delivering a characteristically persuasive and alluring vocal that drew gasps of admiration from the songs authors.

"The song wasn't written for Paul originally and had quite a camp arrangement when I wrote it," Tilbrook explained, "which thankfully we got rid of. It springs from the lyric, which is very simple and I can't help but reflect on Chris's situation. He was taking stock of all the simple things that were nice about his life. We gave it to Paul and again he made it sound ten times better than it would have done."

Despite the fact A&M records spent very little on the promotion of the album, displaying a crushing lack of confidence in the band, the album climbed to #26 on the UK album charts to register only the band's second top thirty album since 1982's Sweets from a Stranger.

The singles unfortunately fared less well. Third Rail (which the band had performed on Later with Jools Holland) could only climb as high as #39 while second single, the album's title track, only reached #73. Despite a memorable performance by the band on Danny Baker's BBC1 chat show third single Loving You Tonight would not trouble the charts at all, although consolation, of a financial nature, arrived when it was chosen for the Four Weddings and a Funeral soundtrack which would prove to be a massive selling record and brought Carrack's golden voice into yet more homes.

By the summer Carrack and Squeeze embarked on a mammoth tour kicking off in Jersey at The Inn On The Park.

"It's loud and fun," Difford wrote in his tour diary that was partially published in Q Magazine at the end of the year, "consisting of seven new songs and a random selection of old chestnuts. The first encore is packed full of them, glowing and pulsating for the eager, sweating crowd. Paul sings and plays with great soul and confidence; it's so great to have him back in the band."

During the tour Paul would sing his two Squeeze singles Loving You Tonight and Tempted and, for the first time in a Squeeze shirt, How Long (Carrack's Soul Cruisin' would also be added to the set-list when the band played Sheffield City Hall).

According to Difford's diary the tour was a highly enjoyable one filled with highlights, notably at Bristol's Colston Hall where the band was joined for its second encore, to the incredulity of the audience, by one Elton John!

"Much to my surprise and delight, my young friend Elton John has chosen to spend his only day off this month in Bristol with me and the band," Difford would scribble. "It is good to see him; he looks very well and happy as ever. Nerves butterfly around my stomach in the build up to the soundcheck as nobody else has met him before. I introduce him and the ice is soon broken; he makes everybody fell very comfortable around him. On stage, the band are on top form. Glenn sings like he's in heaven and generally we hit the audience between the eyes. In the second encore, I introduce the boy saying, We have had many keyboard players in our time- Jools Holland, Don Snow, Paul Carrack - please welcome Elton John. The crowd look at me as if I were joking, a half silence falls on the hall, followed rapidly by a huge roar as he sits at the piano and starts playing the opening riff to Heard It Through The Grapevine. Now too I am in heaven.

"We then launch into I Saw Her Standing There and the place goes nuts. When I look around the stage, the visual orgasm on people's faces was so pleasing to see- not a grumpy jowl in sight. After the show it is hard to contain my excitement; hugs all round. Elton really enjoyed it too, praising Glenn up and down the hall and shaking hands with Paul with true admiration."

The following day, Elton, bless him, went down to his local record shop and bought every copy of Some Fantastic Place they had in stock to give to his friends. Incidentally, the following year Carrack would contribute Hammond Organ to Elton's Made in England album.

"The tour has been a big success," Difford concluded. "We have played the Royal Albert Hall; we have played to over 50,000 people and the shows have been peaking on a regular basis. In Glasgow, it was like being in The Beatles, between songs you had to shout down the microphone to get yourself heard."

Following the UK leg Squeeze crossed the Atlantic for a seven-week tour of North America.

In the New Year February Squeeze were due to make their first ever trip to Japan - but as Paul was committed to some preparatory writing sessions with the Mechanics he had to bow out of these dates and his place was taken by Andy Metcalfe.

By the time Paul was able to rejoin the band for some more American concerts in July Pete Thomas had left Squeeze to rejoin Elvis Costello & the Attractions and their much vaunted reunion.

Bizarrely Thomas was not replaced immediately and the band played some live shows with Paul Carrack playing snare drum in addition to his keyboard duties - at the same time!

As this was not a particularly satisfactory arrangement, Paul recommended his friend Andy Newmark to man the vacant drum stool when the show returned to England, where they were joined on vocals and guitar by singer/songwriter Aimee Mann (Paul would sing Mann's song Stupid Thing during these dates).

With work intensifying on the forthcoming Mechanics album and sundry other projects on his plate Carrack would then bid farewell to Squeeze for a second time.

Although Carrack's second spell in the band (during which the band had also re-re-recorded Tempted for inclusion on the 1994 Winona Ryder movie, Reality Bites) had lasted longer than the first, once again he found himself with too many commitments and not enough time.

One project that Paul seemed particularly keen to be involved in was an unexpected opportunity to work with former Eagles Timothy B. Schmit and Don Felder, with whom Carrack went way back.

"I knew them from our first visit to the States in 1975," Carrack elaborated, "and I met up with Timothy then and over the years when we would go to Los Angeles Timothy and Don Henley would turn up at the gigs and support us so there was always a connection there."

With Eagles leaders Henley and Glenn Frey apparently hemming and hawing about reuniting the band Schmidt and Felder had planned to put together a partial Eagles reunion with guitarist Joe Walsh. When Walsh dropped out of the picture Felder and Schmit decided to see if Paul Carrack wanted to get involved.

"Timothy and I scouted around for another singer," Felder explained. "We tried a couple including Paul Carrack. I wanted one other singer who could play and write, and we eventually settled on Paul and another great guy named Max Carl from the bands .38 Special and Big Dance."

Carrack accepted the invitation and spent much of the summer in Los Angeles writing and recording with the as yet unnamed band, taking with him a wonderful new song he had written with Pete Vale and Jim Capaldi called Love Will Keep Us Alive which was destined to become one of his most successful compositions.

According to Felder the sessions were an absolute pleasure: "It was joy for Timothy and me to work with these guys, compared to some of the experience of recent years. Based at my little studio in Malibu we laughed and had a good time and played really well together."

When the demos were completed Felder attempted to shop them around with a view to getting a record deal: "We put the songs we'd completed on a demo and took them to Irving [Azoff - The Eagles' long time manager] who jumped up and down with excitement." "Hey, Fingers, these are really good!"" he said, with obvious surprise. "I think you might have something here.""

With a major record label deal seemingly now only a phone call away, the band realised it was high time they gave themselves a name. "We'd toyed with a couple of names like Big Sky or Big Party, but nothing seemed to fit," recalls Felder. "We couldn't think of anything that really worked, so we gave ourselves a temporary name - Malibu Men's choir."

Given the individuals involved a record deal seemed to be little more than a formality but ill-fortune struck when the record labels surprisingly passed.

"A week later a fax came rolling off my machine at home," Felder recalls. "There was no preparatory phone call, no attempt at a proper explanation, just two sentences from Irving's office: "We will not be entering into a recording contract with the Malibu Men's Choir. We thank you for your input, but the material you submitted wasn't strong enough." I felt sick to my stomach."

Although all plans for the Malibu Men's Choir were consequently shelved, compensation arrived for Felder and Schmit when The Eagles did decide to get back together for their Hell Freezes Over album and tour. Although Carrack was disappointed by the Choir's failure to launch he too would receive a welcome consolation when the reformed Eagles decided to record Love Will Keep Us Alive.

"Paul did an amazing job on singing that song," Felder later commended. "So Timothy, when we went to do Hell Freezes Over, we were only going to record four new songs and Timothy said, "Aw, I want to sing this song" and Paul had just killed it to me, I thought he'd done a brilliant job."

"Timothy asked me if it would be okay for them to record a version of Love Will Keep Us Alive," Carrack confirms, "and naturally I was delighted."

Carrack was doubly delighted when The Eagles version duly became a massive radio hit, so big in fact that Carrack would receive an award from The American Society of Composers, Authors and Publishers for the most played song of 1995.

As usual Paul had little time to lament missed opportunities because after a four-year absence Mike and the Mechanics were ready to reconvene, performing at The Manor recording studios in Oxfordshire, to mark the twenty-first birthday of Virgin Records in August and finishing what would become Beggar on a Beach of Gold over the late summer and autumn.

For the first time since the band's formation however there was a change in the Mechanics line-up when Rutherford made the awkward decision to tell keyboardist Adrian Lee that he would not be invited to play a full part in the recording.

"Adrian isn't with us this time on keyboards," Rutherford apologised, "and this album is very different because I played a lot of the keyboards on it with the guitar synth and it was very easy getting the sounds I like and many of the songs left this room [Mike's home recording studio] with character, quite a lot of character and sounding quite full. By the time I had done my parts and B.A. Robertson had no problem on the songs we wrote together. Then Paul Carrack obviously played keyboards on the songs that we wrote together and so I wondered what the point of getting Adrian to do it was…."

Although Rutherford had once again written the bulk of the album with Christopher Neil (who would again co-produce) and B.A. Robertson he would also work a lot closer with Paul Carrack than he done previously.

"I have written more with Paul Carrack this time," Rutherford elaborated. "I think that we have improved an awful lot as a writing team second time around."

In the event, however, only two of Carrack's co-writes made it onto the finished album.

The problem appeared to be that Rutherford simply had too many songs from which to fashion the album's final running order, a headache that had been compounded when Genesis's manager Tony Smith suggested doing a couple of cover versions to see if the Mechanics' sound could translate to other people's songs.

Despite the glut of original material available to them, both the cover versions recorded - Stevie Wonder's I Believe (When I Fall In Love, It Will Be Forever) and Smokey Robinson's You Really Got a Hold On Me - would make the album's final cut.

"I am very pleased with this album," Rutherford preened. "To me The Mechanics are more about moods and atmospheres and this album is more like that. I had great difficulty selecting the tracks for this one; there were six that I thought were definite and seven that could be on there and I could chop and choose but then in the middle of all that, Tony Smith suggested that we tried a couple of cover versions. I said, "Why? I've already written nineteen songs I don't think I need any more." But he said; "try it; The Mechanics have a certain sound - just see what you can do with it. If you don't like it you don't have to use it as there are so many Mechanics tracks but it might produce something worthwhile." I went in and recorded a Shadows medley and the Stevie Wonder song When I Fall in Love. That was done fairly straight and Paul sang it on the first day and it sounded good so we put it down there and then with the keyboards and everything."

Carrack's first vocal on the album would be Another Cup of Coffee which marked something of a departure from the band's usual sound. Having rather over-relied on synthetic sounds on previous albums it was good to hear Rutherford come up with something chunky, acoustic and natural sounding.

"He can give you a real good feeling with three simple chords," Tony Banks once remarked about his Genesis colleague and so it proves on the verses (Am, G and F, for the record) and the catchy chorus (F, C and G).

You Really Got a Hold on Me [a cover suggested by Chris Neil], meanwhile presented Mike with the opportunity to realise a long-term goal on a Mechanics album - namely, to have both Pauls singing in tandem.

"I wasn't too sure about that one so we put it down at The Farm and it didn't quite work so we did it differently with a straight 4/4," Rutherford elaborated. "The two Pauls duetted on it after all these years, which was something I had been after and it really came out strong…."

Despite being able to indulge his love of classic soul Carrack seemed confused by the decision to include the cover versions on the album mainly because they were selected at the expense of songs he had co-written: "It was Mike's idea. He calls the shots really. I think it was a bit of an afterthought really. I'm not quite sure why we did it as we had about twenty original songs."

If Carrack was miffed about the decision to relegate some of his co-writes to mere b-sides he proved his point in spades with the highly contemporary sounding album highlight, Over My Shoulder.

Although co-written with Rutherford this betrays more of a Carrack influence to my ears. The whistling solo was particularly inspired and proved to be the sort of song that once heard was almost impossible to dislodge from the noggin.

"Mike and I were writing songs for a new album when we started jamming around a three chord sequence late in the session," Carrack would detail. "We put the cassette player into record and played for about thirty minutes going in all sorts of directions until the tape came to an end. Mike said, "actually I think you had something good happening at the beginning there." When we rolled the tape back to the top there was the whole chorus of Over My Shoulder as it had happened spontaneously."

The moodily atmospheric but lyrically clunky The Ghost of Sex and You, was followed by Carrack's second co-write on the album, Web of Lies, another strong song with some impressive axework from Rutherford and some powerful lead vocals from Paul.

After the rather forgettable A House of Many Rooms (a lengthy mood piece very much in keeping with Rutherford's vision of how his band should sound) Carrack's final lead on Beggar would be I Believe (When I Fall in Love

It Will Be Forever) which would be the more successful of the two covers. Taken from Stevie Wonder's classic Talking Book album Carrack tackles the song respectfully and delivers a superb vocal, even if the decision to fade out robbed him of the chance to let rip as Wonder does on the original's coda and gave the song a sadly unfinished quality.

Both album and lead single Over My Shoulder were released on 13th February 1995 and soon both were riding high in the charts - Shoulder peaking at #12 on the UK singles chart and the album at #9 - a highly respectable return for a band that had been away for four years.

With another successful album and another massive hit single under their belts, the band hit the road in the summer of 1995.

For the tour there was another line-up change when ex-Pink Floyd sideman Gary Wallis replaced Peter Van Hooke on drums.

"Peter [who had played on the album] left because he was producing quite a bit, and I wanted to get someone a bit more constant," Mike explained. "Also, I wanted real drums, and Peter played a lot of electronic drums."

Wallis was impressed by the camaraderie within the Mechanics: "I enjoy The Mechanics most out of all the bands I've worked for," he would say at the conclusion of the tour. "Mike really is the gentleman of pop and we haven't got anything to prove. It's such a great band to be in and as you can see, everyone is totally relaxed, whereas in other bands it can be pretty tough; the artists themselves can be pretty uptight and that goes down the chain of command…"

Having made changes in personnel Rutherford also decided there would be some changes made to the way the band staged their shows.

Inspired by the band's low-key appearance at the Virgin birthday concert, and presumably as a reaction to stadium spectacles that he'd been involved with in Genesis, Rutherford decided he wanted to eschew the bells and whistles and keep things simple: "[The] Virgin gig made me realise that I just want to go to the gig, I don't want all this fuss! It's easy and so much fun and I think we should move towards that. It's much more of a small R&B band or at least more like that, that's my feeling…"

The result was a much more intimate show which proved to be a huge success with the band's fans. Alongside the tracks from the new album and all their hits the Mechanics would also debut a medley of Young's Sad Café hit Every Day Hurts and Ace's How Long, which would go down a storm throughout the entire tour.

The tour kicked off in South Africa, which made the band one of the first to play there since the end of Apartheid. "It was interesting to go there," Carrack remarked, "because it was a new place and they went completely mad and gave us a great reception which kind of set us up and gave us a bit of confidence at the beginning of the tour. We don't get to see much, honestly when we are down there, especially as we rehearsed when we got there, so we didn't get out and about. It still looks pretty grim actually, and we didn't venture far from the hotel because it looked pretty dodgy with the townships and everything, but at least they are trying and I really hope it works out for them."

After their four dates in South Africa (one of which, at Johannesburg's Sandton Towers, was filmed for South African TV) the band headed for Germany before kicking off the UK leg of their tour at Portsmouth's Guildhall on 14th June.

To coincide with the UK leg Another Cup of Coffee was released as a single. Having seen how big a hit Over My Shoulder had been, it made sense to release the only other track on the album that had the same chugging acoustic feel. Although the single was nowhere near as successful (it peaked at #33) it did score them an invite to appear on Top of the Pops on 21st June. As this clashed with a concert appearance at Wolverhapton's Civic Hall the band had to be rushed to the Midlands gig by helicopter.

After the UK leg the band then spent several weeks hopping around mainland Europe - taking in, as if to underline the breadth of their popularity, shows in Ireland, France, Sweden, Denmark, Luxembourg, The Netherlands, the Czech Republic, Austria, Estonia and Belgium where the tour finally wrapped up on 13th August.

Sadly, though, there would be no American tour. Although they would appear at the World Earth Day Festival in Boston in April 1995 it seems their popularity had slumped alarmingly since their Living Years zenith, so much so that Beggar On A Beach of Gold failed to chart at all in the Billboard Top 200, and they were subsequently dropped by Atlantic, their American record label.

Chapter Nine

To capitalise on the UK success of Beggar on a Beach of Gold and Over My Shoulder, Virgin decided to schedule a Greatest Hits compilation for release in March 1996. Naturally, this would mean touring in support of that.

As Paul was shortly to put out another solo album, he was initially reluctant to agree to another Mechanics tour so soon: "As soon as we finished the last tour they asked us to commit to [the Hits] tour because they wanted to put tickets on sale early and I thought, well, I owe it to myself to have a bit of time, but I didn't want to let everybody else in the set up down, and it was up to me and so I said, "alright, I won't do it." And on the positive side, things are going great with this so ... "

Before joining up with the Mechanics again Carrack found time to squeeze in another Genesis-related project, when, again out of the blue, he received a call from the band's former guitarist Steve Hackett, who asked him to sing a couple of songs on his Genesis Revisited album.

Carrack would add his vocals to Déjà Vu (a song started by Peter Gabriel in 1974 and completed twenty-two years later by Hackett) and the Rutherford-penned Your Own Special Way.

"The key was too high - I remember that," Paul chuckled. "One piece was especially good, Your Own Special Way - it is very difficult to sing. Steve is a funny guy. The thing was fun."

After opening for Squeeze during the band's run of London shows in December 1995, Carrack kicked off the New Year with the release of his fifth solo album - Blue Views, recorded the previous May with a crack team of studio veterans - old pal Andy Newmark on drums, the ubiquitous Pino Palladino on bass, Tim Renwick and Robbie McIntosh on guitars, ex-Zombie Rod Argent on keyboards and on backing vocals, Katie Kissoon and Tessa Niles.

Blue Views kicked off with the sublime Eyes of Blue. Penned solely by Carrack the track was originally written for When Saturday Comes - a regrettably fanciful film about Sheffield United reaching the FA Cup Final.

"I was approached by Sheffield-born film producer Jimmy Daley to write a song for a movie he was producing," Carrack elaborated. "The film would be set and made in Sheffield and would star Sean Bean in the lead role. Jimmy described the very basic outline of the story, which is about a young lad who almost wastes a golden opportunity to realise his childhood dream before finally realising the error of his ways and getting his act together. I wrote Eyes of Blue with this scenario in mind but I was mortified to find out, when it was too late, that the lads dream was to play for the dreaded Sheffield United. As a lifelong Sheffield Wednesday fan this caused me untold anguish and embarrassment only slightly relieved when my son Charlie asked "So it's a comedy comedy then Dad?""

Consolation for writing a booster for an admittedly fictional version of his own favourite team's Steel City rivals arrived when Eyes of Blue made the top forty of both the US and UK charts.

If Eyes of Blue was one the best songs he'd ever written, one could easily say the same about both the bulletproof For Once In Our Lives (co-written with Chris Difford) and my own personal favourite on the album, No Easy Way Out.

Boasting a glut of interesting chord changes and an especially tension-building bridge into the chorus, the latter song is sheer R&B bliss and Carrack's persuasive, honey-coated vocal is perfect. Special mention should also be given to Robbie McIntosh who unfurls a careening slide guitar solo that was worthy of George Harrison in his pomp.

Paul changes gear with Oh Oh Oh My My My, a raw soul screamer with which he would occasionally close his live shows, getting the audience to join in on the singalong refrain.

After the slick, breathy Only A Breath Away comes the melancholic ballad, Nothing More Than A Memory. With its Bruce Hornsby-esque piano stylings, heartfelt lead vocal and another delightful guitar solo from McIntosh this was quintessential stuff from Carrack. The remarkable thing is that it had taken him this long to find his true sound.

Although the bluesy Somewhere In Your Heart was comparatively workmanlike Paul couldn't miss with his own version of Love Will Keep Us Alive.

Since the Eagles' version was still relatively fresh in the memory, Carrack sought to ring the changes by using a spontaneous low-key version he had recorded for a pilot TV show, Live From Abbey Road.

Backed delicately by his band this allowed Carrack's voice (which winningly cracks in places) to stand naked as he rings every last drop of emotion from his beautiful ballad. The results are jaw-droppingly good and would render all other versions of this song superfluous, at least for the time being.

Carrack then ups the tempo on the jubilant, easy swinging Always Have, Always Will. With its soupcon of gospel and funky swagger this was another song that couldn't fail to please. The song teases ever so slightly by threatening to pick up the pace at the end of the song. Instead it rather frustratingly fades out.

For Don't Walk Over Me (the second co-write on the album with Chris Difford), Carrack returns to his pop-soul bread and butter, and while the composition itself reiterates Carrack's complete ownership of the form, it's his spine tingling vocal here that really arrests.

While the album closed with a new look at How Long (which still sounded as fresh as the day it was born), some later versions of the albums included a couple of bonus tracks in the shape of an unplugged version of Over My Shoulder and a reverent cover of Curtis Mayfield's People Get Ready. The effortlessness with which he tackled the Mayfield track offered an enjoyable taster of what an album of classic soul covers could sound like should Carrack ever tackle such a project.

Paul was justifiably proud of Blue Views, although he would describe it with characteristic modesty: "It's an honest album. The songs on it I have written over the past few years and I was very keen to record them. It was recorded pretty much live. I only know how to write pop songs - a couple of verses, a chorus and a middle bit. It's not going to change the world, but I hope many people will enjoy it."

"It's just part of my never-ending quest to tell people who I am," he added when interviewed by Billboard magazine, "and what I've done and why they might already like me but don't know who the hell I am. It can be a little frustrating when one's trying to do the solo thing. I'm always starting at square one. But those feelings are tempered by the fact that I've made a career out of music; I can put food on the table, my kids are healthy and fine."

The album was an artistic triumph, arguably the most cohesive and consistent statement of his career so far. One gets a real sense on Blue Views that this was how Carrack had always wanted to present his music - intimate and warm, with melodic songs played by sympathetic musicians on real instruments, rather than computers, synthesizers and drum machines. There's no extraneous studio trickery, every note on the record is there to service the songs, that are supremely well-crafted songs rather than over-produced studio creations.

In addition, everything was redolent of the soul music that continued to inspire him, rather than what record company executives believed passed for soul music, and having gone for a stripped down and highly organic sound the results are extremely authentic; there's a refreshing absence of trends being chased.

Although Blue Views would only peak at #55 in the UK this was his first album to chart in his homeland and the record proved to be hugely successful across mainland Europe, particularly in Spain where he would earn a gold disc.

This was especially impressive given the fact that his record company, IRS, had folded around this time (to become incorporated into Miles Copeland's new label, Ark 21) which meant Blue Views would not be released in America until May 1997 (when Ark 21 finally got around to putting it out). As if to highlight the folly of their delay when they did so For Once in Our Lives became a top five hit on Billboard's Adult Contemporary chart.

In the UK sales of the album were given a boost when both How Long and Eyes of Blue became top forty singles. Carrack would perform the former on Top of the Pops on 11th April 1996 - his first and only solo appearance on the now sadly defunct programme.

"I didn't realise at the time how a little ditty like that would endure all this time and make such a difference," Carrack would say of of his highly durable masterpiece. "It was a complete fluke."

Although a bit more promotion might have brought Blue Views to the wider audience its obvious quality deserved, Carrack had committed himself to the Mechanics' Hits tour. Perhaps acknowledging Carrack's rather selfless sacrifice Rutherford generously allowed Paul to perform Eyes of Blue during the Hits tour.

Prior to the tour Virgin Records released a remixed version of All I Need Is A Miracle and although the single didn't set the charts alight the compilation proved a resounding success - soaring to #3 on the UK album charts.

The Hits tour kicked off in low-key fashion on 28th February at the Island in Ilford, following which the band travelled the length and breadth of the British Isles before signing off with two performances at the Royal Albert Hall on the 18th and 19th of April.

During a break in the Mechanics' tour Paul was able to squeeze in four dates to promote Blue Views with a full band that included Tim Renwick, Toby Chapman and Gary Willis and new boy Dave Bronze on bass.

Even though Bronze had recently been working with Eric Clapton, he was delighted to get the call to work with Carrack.

"That was a big thrill as I have long been a Carrack fan," Bronze enthused. "He is one of the very best vocalists the U.K. has ever produced."

Sponsored by Virgin FM the four dates included a homecoming concert at Sheffield's Leadmill on 2nd April for which Carrack received appropriately ecstatic raves.

"There is no doubt of Paul Carrack's talent as a musician, writer and performer," Peter Morton reviewed, "but to see him perform live with his own band including the likes of Tim Renwick and Gary Wallis was an occasion not to be missed. An almost packed house which not only included the Carrack family and friends but also fans who had all gathered to enjoy a great night of music. And we were not disappointed. Opening up with No Easy Way Out from his current album, it wasn't long before we had the hit, the excellent Eyes of Blue which also appears in the film starring Sean Bean called When Saturday Comes. The rest of Blue Views bar one song followed, during which Paul made a great reference to his playing days in this venue... "The last time

I played here, when it was called The Esquire, was when I was fourteen, so at this rate by the year 2025 I should be playing the Arena!"

In actual fact, Paul would play the arena before the end of the year.

****

His obligations to the Mechanics completed Carrack immediately embarked on another tour, acting as the opening act at various European concerts throughout April, May and the start of June on Sting's Mercury Falling Tour. Accompanied only by Tim Renwick on guitar, Carrack's short sets were well received and his profile was raised considerably due to the fact he would be invited each night to duet with the main attraction on Lithium Sunset - the penultimate show-wrapper-upper - which was widely regarded as the show's highlight.

When Sting took his show to America and Australia Carrack returned to the United Kingdom. Being a huge football fan, Paul Carrack was honoured when he was invited to sing the National Anthem before the Euro '96 match between Scotland and England in front of 72,000 people at Wembley Stadium (Fish from Marillion sang on behalf of the Tartan Army). It was reported that after England's 2-0 win Paul even considered staying with the team to bring them continued luck, but his touring commitments prevented him from indulging this particular dream.

After touring to promote Blue Views, Carrack rejoined Sting in November for the UK leg of his Mercury Falling Tour, appearing at the large arenas in Aberdeen, Glasgow, Newcastle, Cardiff, Birmingham, Manchester, Bournemouth, Brighton, and Sheffield before finishing the tour with six sold-out nights at The Royal Albert Hall - during which Paul was again invited to duet each night on Lithium Sunset and on one night also joined the ex-Police frontman during Let Your Soul Be Your Pilot.

Following a Spanish tour at the start of 1997 Carrack returned to the UK where he was summoned to EMI. During the meeting Carrack received, in his own words, "a big pep talk saying, "yep, Paul get in there and do a new album,"" from the company's big wigs. Suitably encouraged by this vote of confidence Paul went in to the studio to make Beautiful World.

With his sixth solo album in the can awaiting its October release Carrack kept busy during the interim with a brief reunion with Squeeze (the band playing a one-off, private show for a Lottery winner at Chatsworth House) and a clutch of high-profile session dates - contributing organ to Something In The Way You Look Tonight for Elton John's The Big Picture LP (which as the double A-side of Elton's Princess Diana tribute Candle in the Wind '97, would become officially the biggest-selling single ever), Eric Clapton's Pilgrim (recorded in the Autumn of 1997 and released in March 1998), Simply Red's Blue and B.B. King's album of duets, Deuces Wild.

Despite the fact that playing with such famous names was second nature, Paul admitted that he had been nervous working with the seemingly indestructible blues legend: "The one guy I was really nervous meeting and working with was B.B. King, I played the organ and was a vocalist on Deuces Wild in 1997. We were all waiting for him feeling a little nervous as he was coming straight into the studio after flying in from America. You would have expected him to be a bit grumpy or tired but at the age of seventy-five he came in bright eyed and bushy tailed, and he was magic, sang great, and was a funny and humble man."

Given the immense caliber of those invited to duet - among them Clapton, Van Morrison, Dionne Warwick, The Rolling Stones, Joe Cocker, Willie Nelson, Bonnie Raitt to name but a few, it says much for Carrack's standing within his chosen profession that he was the only artist who would duet with the veteran bluesman on two tracks - Bring It Home to Me and Cryin' Won't Help You Babe (with Pink Floyd's David Gilmour on guitar).

For Carrack the sessions were among the most pleasurable of his entire career: "I remember actually one of the sessions was actually on my birthday and he played Happy Birthday for me on the old guitar, in fact I've got a recording of it somewhere and we also did a jam that we put on the album and he called the track Pauly's Birthday Boogie so that's a fantastic memory."

Having finished this burst of session work it was time for Paul to resume his solo career with the release of Beautiful World.

Unfortunately in the time between his big pep talk and the release of the album there had been a sea change at EMI that would have seismic implications for Carrack's solo career.

****

Carrack reportedly got the idea for the Beautiful World album while supporting Sting at the end of 1996. Pleased with the band he had and the vibe they had built up on the road, Carrack felt inspired to capture their chemistry on record. To that end Paul asked Toby Chapman and Gary Wallis to co-produce.

The album gets under way in sprightly fashion with The Way I'm Feeling Tonight, a wonderfully well-crafted pop song co-written with 10cc's Graham Gouldman. Although it was released as a single on 22nd September, a fortnight prior to the album, the record ominously received zero promotional backing from EMI and regrettably failed to chart.

The depth-charging Time To Let Go meanwhile was a much more contemporary sounding effort, built (on the verses) around a drum machine pattern, some keyboard effects, a simple bass pulse and a little 'waka waka' guitar. Although this represented a slight departure from the template he'd established on Blue Views the results are surprisingly effective.

The gospel-infused title track meanwhile would be Paul's personal favourite on the album and one of the best songs of his solo career to date. Despite the obvious strength of the song, it was actually a song that Carrack had seemed initially unsure about.

"I'd had this song lying around half-finished for a while when T-Bone Wolk, came over to stay for a few days," Paul elucidated. "I had always been a bit concerned that the lyric was a little naive but with T-Bone's encouragement we finished the song together."

Normally gospel stylings are the last refuge of a scoundrel but they work here to quite devastating effect. Especially pleasing is the change in tempo at the end of the song over which Carrack offers some splendid vocalising. Again if this had been given to one of the world's soul divas this could easily have become a standard and it was only Carrack's comparatively lower profile that prevented this song from becoming a monster hit, sung each week on the X Factor and American Idol and shows of that ilk by well-scrubbed hopefuls keen to show off their chops.

Carrack changes moods on Perfect Love - a pretty piano ballad, and another song that sounded like the sort of thing Whitney or Celine would have turned into a karaoke favourite, before picking up the pace again with the funky and vibrant You Give Me Something and the R&B infused Satisfied (written with Toby Chapman).

After the atmospheric and Mechanics-like Close To Me, the album then closes in fine style with a trio of treasures: the seductive It Goes Without Saying, which boasts some nice piano licks and a fantastic wailing guitar solo from Tim Renwick, If You'd Ever Needed Someone (a second cousin of Over My Shoulder, written by Carrack and Toby Chapman) and the Ray Charles-esque Some Kinda Love on which Carrack again displays his uncanny knack for writing songs that seem like they've been part of the fabric of soul's history.

Later versions of the album would also include two bonus cuts - a respectful stab at Van Morrison's Into The Mystic and an excellent cover of Percy Sledge's Warm and Tender Love. Although these had apparently been added to the record without Carrack's knowledge or approval, there can have been few fans complaining.

Most male vocalists would be intimidated by tackling songs by Van Morrison or Percy Sledge for fear of suffering by comparison. Carrack though, and with good reason, was evidently untroubled by such insecurities and opens his pipes throughout both as if they had been written especially for him.

After making another exemplary pop soul album, reviews for the album were deservedly complimentary.

"When it comes to comfortable, classy, suburban pop in the lightly soulful mode he is Mr Reliable," applauded Q Magazine. "As befits such an optimistic title, chocolate-box romance of an improbably devotional kind is just about the only thing on the agenda while musically there's a touch of Motown, the odd gospel inflection and nods in the direction of Willie Mitchell and Marvin Gaye; nothing too strenuous. The one defining moment, though, comes with Perfect Love, one of those gushing piano ballads that Whitney, Mariah or Celine would crawl across a roomful of broken glass just to be acquainted with and which, against the odds, he makes sound almost credible. That takes a special kind of talent."

Despite good reviews Beautiful World stiffed in the UK (peaking at a lowly #88) due to a complete lack of support from EMI who promoted the album so poorly that few people were even aware it had been released. In addition they refused to sanction a UK release of the album's potentially game-changing second single - Beautiful World - putting it out only in Continental Europe.

To say that Carrack was miffed at this shabby treatment is a massive understatement. "You see not many people knew that I had a new album out, let alone a single," Carrack cavilled during an interview conducted at the Birmingham Irish Centre on 19th November. "The first single The Way I'm Feeling Tonight was released a couple of weeks before the album and got no airplay or promotional backing from EMI in the UK. The same goes for the album which has done poorly here in the UK."

"I like this album a lot," Carrack added defiantly, "it's got some of my best work on it. Sales are poor simply due to the lack of promotion, I've had no support in the UK from EMI at all! When I signed for EMI the Managing Director [Clive Black] sat me down and talked to me about the great plans he had for me, he was a nice bloke. He had plans to build on the success of Blue Views which I believed in. And when EMI changed Managing Directors [in June 1997 when Clive Black left the company] I tried not to worry."

Unfortunately it had soon become clear that Paul had every reason to worry.

Black's replacement, EMI's former head of media Neil Ferris, it was clear, had no interest whatsoever in Paul Carrack. Meeting for the first time at a record label shindig the oleaginous MD glad-handled the rest of the room, slithering from guest to guest. When he got to Paul Carrack, however, all he could proffer was a brief, limp, eye-contact-free handshake before walking away without saying a word.

"As you can probably imagine," Carrack seethed, "I wasn't going to get on with him."

In fact, Paul would later admit that the instability of his solo career and the money problems caused by Ferris's feckless attitude around this time had made him depressed.

Things had gotten so bad that in one interview in November 1997 Paul asked the journalist to end his article with a request to his fans to write to his record label to complain about the lack of promotion he had received or at least beseech them that he was worth their efforts!

Fortunately Carrack's prolific touring schedule meant he had ample opportunity to get his albums to those reassuringly loyal fans. "The [album has] sold well and fairly steadily at the shows," Paul avowed. "You see, when you buy a copy of the album in a shop I get 80p of that, at the shows I get roughly £5 from each sale."

There was also consolation in the fact that the album was performing strongly in Europe, especially in Spain where Paul had been nominated for, and eventually won, the award for the Best International Male award at their equivalent of the Brits.

For the tours to promote Beautiful World there was a change in personnel when Tim Renwick left Carrack's employ due to the singer's financial difficulties (Renwick was replaced by Mark Hornby). Tim had wanted his regular wage and the budget Paul was on simply could no longer stretch to it.

Things must have been getting desperate because in October, the month prior to the release of Beautiful World, it was widely reported in the press that Carrack had auditioned for the position of lead singer of the Gaelic rock band Runrig, left vacant when Donnie Munro left the band to devote more time to politics, the vocalist having unsuccessfully stood as the Labour Candidate for the Western Isles at the 1997 General Election.

Although it was reported that Carrack and "a mystery Scot" were neck and neck for the job the band decided to turn down Carrack's offer.

"After a series of auditions," the Scottish Daily Record gleefully alleged, "the chart-topping singer was told: All you need is a miracle. The band decided the Gaelic-speaking Scot would cope better with Runrig's hits. And they were worried that Carrack might dump them if Mike And The Mechanics, ever reformed."

In the event the post went to Canadian singer-songwriter Bruce Guthro.

****

Having failed in his bizarre bid to become the new frontman for Runrig (which may or may not have been a publicity stunt) Carrack instead set about touring in support of Beautiful World, including in his itinerary several shows in Spain and Germany.

To coincide with Carrack's return to the UK he and the music industry as a whole received some good news when it was announced that his nemesis Neil Ferris had been relieved of his duties as Managing Director of EMI.

In an interview later in the year Carrack could scarcely conceal his delight: "Unfortunately they had to give him a large payoff to go. He went because it was felt he was making the wrong decisions for EMI, taking them in the wrong direction and trying to get rid of too many areas and concentrate on too few. He didn't deserve the payoff, but I'm very glad he's gone. The new M.D. is fine and runs the company well and how it should be run, considering everyone's tastes and the whole market. I'm much happier with him."

With the new man at the helm Paul started getting more support and promotion for his concerts from Ark 21 and EMI (and a belated Stateside release of Beautiful World) and was now in a much happier frame of mind which showed in his performances, particularly during his three-night run of shows at Ronnie Scott's in Birmingham during the second city's jazz festival, which included for the first time in his career, an hour-long solo set.

Although he had stated how much he had been enjoying being a solo act the tail end of November 1998 saw Paul return to Mike and the Mechanics to record the group's fifth album.

Interviews with Carrack suggested once again that he was initially reluctant to once again put his solo ambitions on pause.

"I was very apprehensive about it a few weeks ago," Carrack stated prior to rejoining his bandmates, "but now I'm beginning to feel more at ease with it. I know once I'm in there everything will be back to normal, but when you have long breaks from it and are doing solo projects like I am, you find it strange to get back in to."

Although Rutherford had already written some songs with his usual sidekicks Chris Neil and B.A. Robertson the bulk of the album would be written with Carrack and Young. Carrack and Rutherford would jam together on guitar and keyboard, whilst Paul Young would suggest rhythmic and melodic ideas. The lyrics would usually be the last thing added, often as not inspired by the mood of the music.

A total of eighteen songs were written during the Mike & the Mechanics sessions (which would later become more fondly known as M6 as it was the band's sixth album, including the Hits compilation), but due to time constraints only the twelve tracks that appeared on the album actually made it into the recording studio.

The Mechanics were now effectively a studio trio, with Carrack and Rutherford tackling the instrumentation between them - Rutherford on guitars and bass and Carrack on keys and, for the first time as a Mechanic, on drums.

There was also changes in the production team with Rutherford tackling the production duties largely on his own (in the absence of Chris Neil), assisted by Genesis producer Nick Davis and Matthew Vaughan.

Since tour dates had been finalised before the album had been completed the band had to work to a tight deadline of March 1999, but although Rutherford felt this compromised the writing process it did lend the album an immediacy and prompted the band to rely a great deal less on studio wizardry than they had done in the past.

One of the exceptions to that was the album's lead single, Now That You've Gone. Described by Rutherford as "our attempt at a dance track," the track was produced by Mark Taylor and Brian Rawling, the men responsible for Cher's Believe which had been a monster hit the year before. The hook of that song had been Cher's vocals fed through a vocoder and the keyboard and drum beats du jour and both were appended to this Mechanics track in a somewhat brazen and possibly ill-judged attempt to recreate the success of the earlier hit.

"It began life as any normal Mechanics song," Mike detailed. "But I gave [Taylor and Rawling] the original tapes, and they did something different with it, which was good for the band."

The result was inevitably a Mechanics / Believe hybrid and although the results are a bit Eurovision for my tastes the single did creep into the U.K. top forty - peaking at #35.

Although M6 lacked a truly great stand-out track the album wasn't without highlights, such as the circa 1966 Beatley Ordinary Girl, and the strident When I Get Over You (both sung by Young) as well as the guitar driven and harmony-rich What Will You Do and the Byrds-y Did You See Me Coming? (both sung by Carrack).

All in all M6 was a consistent and pleasant soft rock album and although it could be argued that the world didn't really need a new Mechanics album in 1999 the album performed surprisingly well.

Buoyed by some strong reviews (the album garnered an uncharacteristically generous four stars out of five from Q Magazine), M6 would climb as high as #12 on the UK album charts which showed just how loyal their fanbase remained, a fact underlined by the packed theatres at which the band would play on their summer tour of the UK (during which the band was augmented by Gary Wallis on drums and new guitarist Jamie Moses who replaced Tim Renwick).

After a performing an album premiere in front of a small invited audience of media representatives and competition winners on 10th May at London's Hanover Grand club (during which, at various times, Carrack displayed his versatility by playing keyboards, acoustic guitar and bass) the tour proper began three days later at York's Barbican Theatre and stretched through to the end of June.

Though the Mechanics did play a couple of festivals in Germany where their following remained solid, Rutherford would reveal they had found their way barred from most of the summer festivals that year.

"Well we normally do the festivals but this year the festivals have gone a bit younger," Rutherford lamented, "they've gone for the young bill of The Manic Street Preachers, Placebo, that sort of band and we are a bit cold. It's always hard coming back to the Mechanics. It's always a bit cold until they hear some music and trying to pre-sell the Mechanics is impossible until they hear some music and then they go 'oh yeah' and attitudes change..."

The band then reconvened at the start of July for a couple of nights at Dublin's Olympia Theatre and an appearance at the T In The Park Festival in London's Hyde Park. The Mechanics were then invited to support Celine Dion at Sheffield's Don Valley Stadium on 6th July and at Wembley Stadium (on 10th and 11th July) before rounding off their touring activities for the year with a slot supporting Rod Stewart at Manchester City's Maine Road football stadium on 22nd July.

Although they weren't to know it at this stage Mike and the Mechanics would never be the same again.

Chapter Ten

Disillusioned by the shabby treatment he had received from EMI, Paul concluded, as he entered his fifth decade in the music business, that working for major labels was no longer for him.

Encouraged by his old friend Peter Van Hooke, Paul consequently grasped the nettle and decided to set himself up as an independent artist, forming his own record label, Carrack-UK.

"At the end of the 1990s I realised the traditional deal with a traditional record label was not necessarily the best option for me," Carrack elaborated. "By then I had a pretty good idea what needed to be done and it was just a case of seeing if I could bring all the parts together. It was a risk - I could have buried my own career - but I am glad I made the decision when I did."

His first album as an independent artist would be Satisfy My Soul, which would be a solo album in every sense of the word. Recorded in his home studio in Hertfordshire, Carrack wrote, produced and performed virtually every note on the album entirely on his own, joining a very select group of artists who can boast such self-sufficiency.

"I have a little studio at home and I started recording as I was writing it with a view to recording the material over again," Carrack explained. "But I found when I went back to what I'd done that it had a certain feel to it. So instead of drafting in other producers and artists I kept it the way it was."

After periods of, by his own admission, allowing outside producers to impose their often unsuitable sound on his material, and years of wildly ill-informed interference from record label apparatchiks and their accountants, the decision to rely on and trust solely his own instincts was a long overdue move.

"On my early solo albums," Paul asserted, "I would definitely not trust my own judgement, I tended to let producers and people have free reign. I just thought they knew better than me. It wasn't until I started the label that I began to say, "You know what? I'll do it how I want to do it and hope that people like it.""

"I think [Satisfy My Soul is] a true representation of me and what I want to do," Paul added. "This time I trusted my own judgement. The album has my stamp on it, my feel. It's as honest an album as I've made and people who like what I do will enjoy it. That's all that matters. I'm not after world domination - I just want to enjoy myself musically."

Guided by his own muse Satisfy My Soul would turn out to be a much more mature and thoughtful record.

"At one time, I would have wondered about getting relaxed and mellow," Carrack stated, "but let's face it, I'm an older chap. It was great doing it in the home environment and not having somebody breathing down my neck telling me how it ought to be done. I haven't had happy experiences with record companies recently but anyone who is not a Number One priority at a record company will normally have a bleat about it.

"When I started writing the songs, it was in a very relaxed mode, but also a productive mode. I would say I go into the studio Monday to Friday, Saturdays and Sundays I don't because I think you need a break. I work pretty hard. The attitude with this album was that I was on a bit of a roll anyway with my writing, I was just letting it come out, not being too self-critical. I don't self-edit myself too much. I don't sit there and say, "oh that's too mellow," or "that's too Sam Cooke, that's not allowed." I just let it come out.

"I think I've earned the right to enjoy what I do now. I'm not trying to ram anything down anybody's throats but anyone who knows what I do will realise that it is a better representation of myself than I've managed so far."

"Most of the sort of things I've been involved with have been collaborations," Carrack acknowledged, "in the case of Mike and the Mechanics, quite unusual collaborations. When I sing I only know how to sing one way but with Mike and Mechanics, it's a different setting. It's a shame but the soulful aspect of my work, which is what I'm really about has got lost a bit along the way."

If Satisfy My Soul was therefore an attempt to redress this musically, the album would also be more personal in tone lyrically, touching as it did on such private autobiographical matters as his childhood and his friends and family.

"I think in the past, I might have been more guarded about those kind of things because I'd worry about being shot down in flames," Carrack mused. "Going this independent route, you can do what you want and hope that people who don't like what you do ignore you rather than have a go at you."

The album kicked off with the sleek Satisfy My Soul co-written with Chris Difford, which, on first listen, one could be forgiven for thinking this was a cover of a Sam Cooke classic. One thing that's worth noting with no small amount of admiration is the way Carrack reveals himself to be an instinctive master of multi-part harmony on this track.

Having stated his intention to make, "a grown up record ... that represented me and what I was about" Together and Where Would I Be would be a brace of sincere tributes to his wife, Kathy, celebrating the long and happy marriage they had shared. The lyrics might have been personal but the messages in both were universal, ones that would undoubtedly have touched a nerve with Carrack's demographics.

My Kind, meanwhile, continues the theme of paying loving tribute to his family, this time to his youngest daughter Merrilee. My Kind would turn out to be one of the most heartfelt and moving songs of Paul's career and makes one think that had he been born in another era and on another continent Carrack could easily have been a staff writer for Motown. Frankly, whoever did his publishing should have gotten this over to Smokey Robinson with all due haste.

Carrack would reveal that the song had actually been written around the time of Merrilee's birth: "While all the other songs are brand-new, this has been going around my head for years. I wrote it for my daughter Merri when she was just a baby - and she's fourteen now!"

After the bluesy Inspire Me (on which Carrack shows himself to be a fine electric guitarist), another lush tribute to his wife on The Only One (co-written by Chris Difford) and How Wonderful (a joyful celebration of the pleasures of life) came came the harder-edged Running Out Of Time.

An album highlight, Running Out Of Time boasted one of the best lyrics of Carrack's entire career. A South Yorkshire take on Bryan Adams' Summer of '69, Paul details his long musical journey, name-checking the days when he would beat cardboard boxes in his parents attic, putting records on the Dansette and waving his brother John goodbye at Sheffield train station on his way to Germany.

Another fine groove was the funky Better Then Nothing that would prove to be a live crowd-pleaser. Carrack's drumming displays a tremendous sense of feel on this track and the slinky saxophones (played by Steve Beighton) are also a treat.

The album closes with Time Passes, a mid-paced love song with a chugging acoustic guitar setting that suited Carrack well and the funky Make Your Mind Up, which like Better Then Nothing would prove to be another live favourite.

Later versions of the album would also include three bonus tracks: re-recordings of Silent Running and Eyes of Blue and a version of Bring It On Home To Me which featured BB King and Jools Holland (the following year Carrack would repay the favour by lending his lead vocals to It's So Blue on Holland's Small World Big Band album).

The album was an unqualified triumph, one that allowed Carrack's soulful sound to fulminate with a newfound brightness and punch. In short, it was a record of which Paul could justifiably be proud and even a decade later he was still naming Satisfy My Soul as his favourite of his own albums.

"Hopefully it showcases my strengths as a songwriter," he said. "The material's all about relationships and family values, but there's no point in faking it - I am that family guy, trying to raise four kids. I've been making music all my life and often made it quite difficult for myself. But I'm at a point where I just want to enjoy my musicality and I have the technical resources and the stability to be able to follow my instincts more confidently."

The decision to form Carrack-UK was rewarded when Satisfy My Soul climbed to a highly respectable chart placing of #63 - his highest charting album in the UK since Blue Views and some of the best reviews of his career.

"Essentially a family man amazed to have found himself, decades on from the initial rush of Mersey Beat," Colin Harper congratulated in Mojo Magazine, "a survivor of the cruel ebbs and flows of musical fashion, this is Carrack saying, "No More rock star pretences - this is who I am and what I have to say. "What he has to say will, in fact, strike chords with thousands of everyday people whose monochrome lives take constant solace in sunlit dreams. Classic soul and pop values deliver here a sound more organic and less bombastic than Carrack's work with Mike & The Mechanics... this Album is the sound of the small man coming through and doing the do with class and dignity."

Since Paul could now longer call upon the sort of distribution network that a major record label can boast he realised that the best and most profitable way to get his record to his fans was to tour extensively. To do that Paul needed a new band and he found one in Sheffield club band, the Dynamite Brothers, that comprised Steve Beighton on sax, Paul Copley on keyboards, bassist Jeremy Meek, guitarist John Robinson and drummer Dean Dukes. The band would play such an integral part in establishing Carrack as a solo touring act that he's been with them ever since.

The Satisfy My Soul tour would prove to prove to be Carrack's most extensive solo tour to date, kicking off in the Spring of 2000 and continuing off and on across the UK and Europe until well into the following year.

The tour had barely begun, however, when Carrack received the tragic news that his Mike & The Mechanics band mate Paul Young had died at his home in Hale, Greater Manchester. Despite all efforts to resuscitate him, Young died of a heart attack in the early evening of 15th July, leaving behind a wife, Pat, and three children. He was just fifty-three.

Paul was understandably devastated to lose such a close friend and colleague (the Mechanics had been due to play a couple of festivals in Scandinavia at the end of the month): "The news about Paul was a great shock," Paul would say in tribute. "I always say that Paul was a natural born star who never shone brighter than when he was performing on stage and making people happy. We called him the 'King of rock n roll' and although we will all miss him greatly it is even harder for his family. May he rest in peace."

"We are all shocked and devastated by Paul's death," added Mike Rutherford. "He had a fantastic voice, one of the best rock voices of this generation, and aside from his musical talent he had such an infectious enthusiasm for the business. Paul loved performing. We all thought he would be singing in fifty years time."

Although he hadn't been the most prolific composer his energetic stage presence and natural showmanship had been without doubt the band's live focal point. No one would argue that he had always been, in effect, the Mechanics' frontman.

Fittingly, a tribute concert, entitled Forever Young, would be held in December at the Manchester Apollo. After a set apiece from The Toggery Five (with whom Young had played back in the 1960s), the SAS Band (Young's last project), and Sad Café, The Mechanics topped the bill with a set that comprised Get Up, Another Cup Of Coffee, Silent Running, The Living Years and Over My Shoulder, which were followed by All I Need Is A Miracle and Word Of Mouth (with Chris Thompson singing the latter). Between the songs all the musicians shared fond memories of and stories about their departed friend while the backdrop behind them screened images of the man for whom they had gathered to honour.

Although bittersweet and emotional the night proved to be a fitting celebration of the life of such a talented man, who would be dearly missed by his friends, family and, of course, fans of the Mechanics. In fact, his tragic passing left the future of the Mechanics hanging in the balance.

****

The Satisfy My Soul tour, meanwhile, continued to roll on, playing to packed houses wherever it went, culminating on 4th May 2001 with an unforgettable sold out show at the Royal Albert Hall to mark Carrack's fiftieth birthday.

"It's always been my favourite venue and I'd played there many times with different bands but this time we thought we'd push the boat out," Carrack explained. "It was my fiftieth birthday so we thought we'd make a thing of it and we did fill out the Albert Hall but I did have the support of a lot of my friends - Mike came down and the guys from Squeeze, B.A. Robertson and Nick Lowe; we had so many people it was great, it was a good party..."

Entitled 'Paul Carrack in Good Company' the night would prove to be one of the highlights of his career.

After being introduced by Radio 2 DJ and long-time Carrack cheerleader Ken Bruce (whom Paul joked had been worth the £10 he'd been paid to emcee), Paul and his band opened with a superlative Silent Running and an appropriately titled The Way I'm Feeling Tonight.

Switching to electric guitar Carrack then wowed the Hall with a touching performance of My Kind (which he dedicated to his daughter who was in attendance along with her three siblings), a funky Better Than Nothing and a stunning version of Love Will Keep Us Alive.

At this point Paul introduced his first guest, former Zombies' organist Rod Argent who accompanied Carrack on a soulful version of She's Not There, a show-stopping version of Hoagy Carmichael's Georgia on My Mind and Van Morrison's Into the Mystic.

Next up to the oche was Paul's great mate, a besuited Nick Lowe who sang (What's So Funny 'Bout) Peace, Love and Understanding. Although Lowe's appearance was all too brief Carrack made sure there was no time for the audience to grieve by heading straight for his piano to launch into an immaculate solo trio of Eyes of Blue, The Only One and a haunting cover of Mathilde Santing's Marie.

Switching to acoustic guitar Carrack then introduced his next guest - former featherweight boxing champion of the world, Barry McGuigan, who stunned the audience with a note-perfect version of the Mike and the Mechanics number Whenever I Stop.

"He came and sang on stage and he's actually got a really good voice," Carrack quipped. "I certainly wasn't going to ask him to leave."

Next up was B.A. Robertson, who performed a delightful, slower version of the Mechanics' song All the Light I Need, accompanied by Paul who played piano and sang a verse himself.

At this point Paul's band returned to the stage and launched into Satisfy My Soul which proved to be the perfect opportunity to introduce the song's co-writer as the next guest, whom Paul billed as "definitely one of the best lyricists ever to come out of this country" - Chris Difford.

With Difford smiling beatifically throughout Carrack joined his frequent collaborator on acoustic guitar for a sweet version of their song How Wonderful and if that wasn't magical enough Paul then introduced 'Mr Golden Tonsils,' and a visibly excited Glenn Tilbrook bounded onto the stage. As Squeeze had broken up in 1999 reuniting the band's two mainmen was quite a coup.

Backed superbly by Carrack's band the three friends treated the audience to Up the Junction and Hourglass which sandwiched a roof-raising rendition of Tempted.

At the end of their delightful cameo Difford, Tilbrook and Carrack shared an endearing group hug. Without giving the audience the chance to pause for breath out strolled Mike Rutherford to a wall of appreciative applause, for a foot-tapping version of Over My Shoulder and an appropriately moving singalong-a-Living-Years (with B.A. Robertson on the piano), which sent the audience into raptures and prompted another group hug.

After performing If You'd Ever Needed Someone Carrack then took a short vocal breather and allowed Paul Copley to take the spotlight and get the audience shaking their ass on Some Kinda Love, while Carrack comped alongside on the organ. Carrack then completed the night with an audience participative How Long.

Despite performing a set lasting over two hours, the audience were clearly in no mood to allow the party to end and their deafening calls for more coerced Paul and the band to return for two encores - a funky Make Your Mind Up and a raucous cover of Sly and the Family Stone's Dance to the Music.

At the end of the concert Carrack remained on stage for several minutes, soaking up the genuine cataract of good will and admiration from the crowd and no doubt reflecting how far he had come since those days in Sheffield bashing his drums along to Gerry and the Pacemakers and dreaming of nights like this. If he was basking in the glow of selling out the Albert Hall as a solo star he had every right to do so. After all, there can't be many better ways to celebrate turning fifty.

At the conclusion of the Satisfy My Soul tour Paul Carrack released his first DVD - Paul Carrack in Concert, filmed live at the Shepherd's Bush Empire which provided a celluloid documentation of Carrack's evolution into a much more confident performer, as Paul himself acknowledged: "It's important for me to be my own man, and I've fought long and hard to establish this thing I've got now. I think I'm currently writing good stuff and I'm doing good dates. I get more of a kick out of performing now, in a way, because I don't get so scared as I used to. I feel a lot more comfortable being the big cheese up the front there. I never really had the stomach for that before."

****

While still touring in support of Satisfy My Soul, Carrack began the early stages of his next album, Groovin' - a labour of love on which he paid tribute to the artists who had most influenced him as a musician.

"One sunny day back in June 2001," Paul explained, "I was messing about in my studio as usual when I found myself gazing out of the window singing "Groovin' on a sunday afternoon" remembering my days as a young lad in Sheffield, gigging around the dancehalls and clubs, dreaming of sitting behind a big old Hammond B3 organ and becoming a Young Rascal."

Much to Carrack's credit, he eschewed the easy and somewhat cynical route of selecting songs the world and his wife had heard a million times and instead opted for a more eclectic mixture.

Described by Carrack as an album of "songs I have been singing in the bath for the last thirty years," the album would contain the Isley Brothers' Harvest For The World, Bobby Hebb's Sunny, the Motown classic Too Busy Thinking About My Baby, Van Morrison's Crazy Love, The Four Tops' Baby I Need Your Lovin', Dionne Warwick's Walk On By, Junior Walker's What Does It Take?, Burt Bacharach's Anyday Now (which featured a fine string arrangement by Paul's friend Rod Argent), Percy Sledge's Cover Me, Lou Johnson's Allen Toussaint-penned With You In My Mind, Bill Withers' Ain't No Sunshine, The Young Rascals Groovin' and Carole King's You've Got A Friend.

"For me, that's the greatest era of pop music," Carrack enthused. "They're all just great songs to sing. It was painless, really - all the graft's been done by the writers. There are a couple of tracks from Van Morrison's Moondance, which is a particular favourite of mine - in the days when you just had three albums in your collection, that was one of them: I know every note on that record backwards. I have big respect for Van, not just as an artist, but for the way he's always done his own thing, regardless of what anybody else thought. I just wish I'd taken a leaf out of his book sooner."

For many reviewers the idea of tackling several sacrosanct soul classics was a brave one, after all cover version albums don't always turn out well. "Well, why not?' Carrack retorted, keen to point out that he'd been a card-carrying fan of this music since he'd been a nipper and he'd more than paid his dues. "I think it's fair enough to do a version of a song you like, in this context. I grew up playing those songs in soul bands in Sheffield when I was still at school."

The album would prove to be another strong seller when it was released in the Autumn of 2001, further vindicating Carrack's decision to go it alone: "It's fantastic having my own label, I wish I'd sussed it out a bit sooner, it's the only way to go really. Things have changed, there's a much better infrastructure there for doing it independently. I think it's absolutely marvelous, I can just sense the support I've got. Every day I'm getting letters from the people saying they like it. It's brilliant - I love it. Plus, I'm getting the lion's share of the money and I can make my own decisions. If I want to make an album of covers, I can do it, I don't have to sit around having meetings."

Paul was evidently pleased with the album. So much so that he later re-packaged and re-issued the album as Still Groovin' which generously included with five bonus tracks - Into The Mystic, People Get Ready, Warm and Tender Love, It's Growing and I Wish It Would Rain - and a bonus six-track DVD of live performances.

It was clear that Carrack was becoming increasingly confident in his role as bandleader and captain of his cottage industry, certainly confident enough to deflect questions about when Mike and the Mechanics were getting back together which many lazy journalists always seemed to want to ask him. Paul, at least at this stage, appeared to believe the tragic death of Paul Young had effectively quashed any desire he personally had to reform.

"We miss Paul like mad," Carrack rationalised. "Personally, that's why I would find it very difficult to do anything else as Mike & The Mechanics. It wouldn't seem right to me. I know Mike Rutherford is quite keen to do something, and we've written a few songs together, but I would feel uncomfortable, I think. That's my feeling at the moment anyway. Paul Young was a major part of the band, and it would seem very weird without him. You can never say never, but to be honest I'm so involved with having to keep my thing afloat and ticking over, I don't give it a lot of thought."

Certainly Paul had enough on his plate as it was - not only his own busy touring schedule but a whole raft of interesting and rewarding sidelines.

On Valentine's Day 2002 Carrack received an unexpected treat when he was invited up on stage at the Shepherd's Bush Empire to join one of his heroes, Sam Moore, to sing Wrap it Up.

"I met Sam a few years ago when he was over in London," Paul bubbled. "I was major major fan and I was very very honoured that he actually knew who the hell I was and he was aware of some of my stuff so to meet him was fantastic and he got me up in stage and I sang with him which was brilliant."

During this period Paul also found time to act as a special guest mentor on Operacion Triunfo, the Spanish version of X Factor, filmed at Barcelona's Acadamia. The phenomenally successful show, which went out live twenty-four hours a day on its own special channel, achieved the biggest viewing figures for any show of its kind worldwide - a whopping seventy per cent audience share!

"I was invited over as a guest to go on the show meet some of the kids and talk to them about my career and some of their questions," Carrack elaborated, "and I sat round at the piano and sang a few things with them and that was it, that was the sum total of my involvement to be absolutely honest with you. I'm not usually a big fan of those kind of talent contest kind things but I think the one in Spain ... I liked it better than the English versions, it was a little bit less harsh, a little bit less cut throat and not only that but the kids actually had a lot of talent."

One contestant who evidently caught Paul's attention was Joan Tena with whom he would duet on a Castilian Spanish-language version of Eyes of Blue (Mirada Azul) in 2003 which can hardly have hurt Carrack's already massive popularity in that country, and also showed that he could sound fantastic even when singing phonetically.

Still the accolades kept coming when in 2003 Paul accepted an invitation to become a member of ex-Beatle Ringo Starr's latest All-Star Band for a series of American concerts.

The All-Star band enterprise had first started in 1989. Although the drummer had sung lead on several Beatles classics and had scored a fistful of top ten singles on both sides of the Atlantic it was fair to say that his catalogue alone was not sufficient to sustain a full concert. As a result Ringo had formed a succession of touring supergroups with other legends and they would take it in turns, revue style, to perform their hits.

"For me it works as a great formula," Ringo explained, "it's just really a great way for me to do it. If you look at all the bands I've put together, it's an incredible array of musicians, all these different people. Everyone has hit records, hit songs. The show consists of me upfront and then I go back behind the kit and support the others. It's just good music and I'm having a lot of fun and that's what it's all about - great music and fun."

The 2003 vintage was the eighth version of the All-Star Band. Joining Carrack for the three-month jamboree was Sheila E. (Prince and the Revolution), Colin Hay (Men At Work) and John Waite. Each performer would be allotted three songs (in Carrack's case, How Long, Tempted and Living Years), peppered throughout a set that would also include such Beatles songs as Honey Don't, Boys, Act Naturally, Yellow Submarine, Don't Pass Me By and With a Little Help From My Friends, as well as both of Ringo's American #1 singles (You're Sixteen and Photograph) and an ensemble version of Here Comes The Sun.

Carrack admitted his time playing in the same band as a Beatle was the realisation of "a boyhood dream." He also revealed that he had had to turn Ringo down on a couple of occasions: "I've been up for doing it for a couple of years, but for one reason or another it didn't happen [due to clashing tour dates], and fortunately he asked me again this year. And when a Beatle calls, you have to say yes!"

The tour kicked off on 24th July 2003 at Toronto's Casino Rama (a date which was recorded and later released as a DVD and CD) and eventually encompassed thirty-two dates before drawing to a close at Humphrey's in San Diego on 7th September.

"It was just a fantastic experience," Carrack remarked at the end of the tour. "It wasn't the most challenging thing I've done musically, it was basically Ringo likes to go out and have fun once a year and forms a band of all-stars you've got to have three hits to be in the band, you've got to take it in turns and Ringo does his, and it's just fun. And you are so well looked after it's just ridiculous. I'd do it again."

At the conclusion of the tour, as a mark of appreciation, Ringo gave Paul a rare Hofner Verithin JS semi-acoustic guitar (of which only fifty had ever been produced).

****

In between touring with his own band and with Ringo and tutoring Spaniards, Paul somehow found the time to write and record a new album, It Ain't Over. As with Satisfy My Soul and Groovin', Carrack once again largely wrote, produced and performed the whole thing himself.

"It's almost all me again," he confirmed prior to the album's release, "apart from the horns on about five tracks, and the strings on a couple of tracks, which were played by Wired Strings, who appear on Top Of The Pops quite a bit these days: they're young and gorgeous and they actually like pop music, so they play with feeling, which helps - sometimes it's hard to get the right performance out of older string players. This one's a bit more upbeat than Satisfy My Soul, which was more of a mature, reflective album. That's largely the result of doing so many gigs - and I know a lot of these songs will work really well live, too."

It Ain't Over kicks off with the wistful She Lived Down the Street. With lyrics by Chris Difford the song deals with two childhood sweethearts, and charts their loving life together. Carrack composed a wonderful acoustic guitar chord sequence that Difford's usual writing partner Glenn Tilbrook would have been very proud to have written, making the song sound very Squeeze-like and therefore quite anomalous in terms of this album (although no less good), which hereafter heads into blissful, classic soul territory with, frankly, stunning results.

If She Lived Down the Street, was a Squeeze song in all but name I've Got Nothing to Lose could almost be the best song Al Green never released and was precisely the sort of thing Carrack's fans loved about their hero - his ability to write smooth, soul-infused songs that few of his peers could match for authenticity.

Equally as good was the album's sinuous title track, which Carrack revealed had been inspired by Sheffield Wednesday's unsuccessful battle battle against relegation in 2003, adding that the song was also "a statement of intent with regard my own life and career" - "I won't ever quit," Carrack sings, vocalising the determination that continued to drive him, "I ain't gonna stop, keep on going 'til I drop."

Carrack again changes tack on Happy to See You Again. Although Carrack can't suppress his soulful side, he manages to create a wonderfully rich mid-sixties-cum-Motown hybrid replete with a sumptuous and Beatley middle eight. Fittingly, the song would go on to become a Top Forty hit on the Billboard Adult Contemporary Chart when it was released as a single.

Even the light reggae of Where Did I Go Wrong fails to throw Carrack offbeam. Now I personally can't think of a single white reggae artist I don't despise but Carrack gets the balance here just right, helped by an unstoppable chorus and fine work on the saxophone from touring mainstay Steve Beighton.

Although Carrack clearly didn't need assistance writing lyrics, his songwriting partnership with Chris Difford always seemed to bring out the best in the pair of them and their second collaboration on the album was the beautiful Empty Space, a mid-paced smoocher, that one could easily imagine Otis Redding singing.

One Small Step (written with lyrical assistance from B.A. Robertson) meanwhile was a perfect example of Carrack's almost effortless ability to compose suberb ballads that the world should know and love. On it Carrack is largely accompanied merely by his own piano and a tasteful, exponentially swelling string arragement over which he delivers a classy lead vocal. Resisting the temptation to give it the full power ballad treatment, Paul instead mines the subtler nuances in the melody in a way that Mamselles Carey and Houston never had the skills to explore, preferring to needlessly showboat in a way that Carrack has always had the good taste to eschew.

Equally gorgeous was Forever which was the sort of song the Walrus of Love, Barry White, might have essayed during his seventies pomp, albeit with a deeper voice.

Once again showing his protean ability to shift between genres Carrack then offers a fine slice of lean, dirty funk on Never Too Late, and the sultry, horn heavy Just a Little Lie both of which which would prove live highlights in the tours to come and on which Steve Beighton again excels.

The album concludes with the stunning Ain't No Love on which Carrack duets with himself to stunning effect. Although the fizzy guitars gave Ain't No Love a very modern feel the song sounds so much like a Sam and Dave number that I had to toothcomb the album's credits and Google to double check that it wasn't.

In my opinion with It Ain't Over, Carrack finally painted his masterpiece. This was stunning sophisticated pop and soul music that's all dressed up and without a hair out of place. Whereas in the past there was injustice that Carrack's tracks hadn't been heavily rotated on every adult contemporary radio station in the English speaking world it was now bordering on a criminal offence.

The album was warmly received by the critics: "With this album, Paul Carrack further emancipates himself from the things that used to determine his career," wrote one journalist. "He knows where he wants go to musically and he knows what he likes. It may be doubted that he will ever enjoy commercial success, particularly since the current mainstream does not leave much space for Carrack's style of music, much less for a singer who does not come from a casting show or spends less than four hours styling himself per day. But then you never know. Paul himself is probably less interested in chart success than in making the music he enjoys and bringing it to the people in a way he enjoys."

Once again Carrack took to the road in support of his new album. Despite the fact that he was now fifty-three it was clear he still couldn't resist the lure of live performance.

"I don't know why I still perform, I wish I knew. I could probably carve myself a little living out of song writing and play golf and have a less stressful life. I figure I spent a lot of time learning how to do it and I believe I'm as good if not better than I've ever been. And with my band all based in my home town of Sheffield I think we've got a good thing rolling and long may it reign. If it gets to the point that I feel I'm not giving good performances or I'm going through the motions or whatever I will definitely pack it in. But at the moment I honestly feel I'm doing well and the response I get from the audiences by and large is very, very supportive and I think they do want me to continue... It's nice to go out there and do what you think is a good job and then get your back slapped at the end of the night with big beaming smiles from people going home happy -- it feels worthwhile. "

For his It Ain't Over tour, that kicked off in the Autumn of 2003, Carrack decided to mix things up a little.

"In this year's tour," Paul explained, "we've given things a slightly different twist as the first set is a kind of acoustic one with some different treatments of some of the well known songs and some of the older songs. The second set is with a full band and has a few more whistles and bells and things like back projections and all that stuff."

Ahead of the tour Paul paid tribute to his backing band: "It has been a revelation. I have worked with some of the best musicians in the world, but the vibe I get with these guys is unique. They are very committed, love doing it and they can play."

"It really works great, I love the fact that they give me one-hundred per cent support. In the past, I've always had to hastily assemble a band of session players, but I definitely feel the situation we've got now is far more like a real band. It really gels now, and I'm happy with that. I go back to Sheffield to rehearse, we have our own facility where we store our equipment, so it's more practical for me to go there. My band want to play for me, you know, and when they're not playing for me they do their own gigs as the Dynamite Brothers, doing a different repertoire completely. People are coming to see me because they already know the music, to a large extent. I think they've finally put together who I am and everything. I don't feel as if I'm being hyped up and sticking my neck out, as if I've got to live up to anything, I feel quite good about being out there."

In October, though, Carrack was dealt a body blow when thieves stole his tour van from the car park of outside the Brewers Fayre Travel Lodge in Brampton, Cambridgeshire, where he and his band were staying before a gig.

The white Mercedes van was found abandoned two days later but most of the equipment was missing, including guitars, drums, keyboards and PA systems.

Paul was naturally devastated to lose not just thousands of pounds worth of kit but also some treasured instruments. "A lot of the instruments are my private possessions and hold great memories for me," he lamented. "The

Hofner guitar was given to me during the summer when I was touring with Ringo Starr."

Although the tour was thankfully able to resume after just two cancelled (and later rescheduled) gigs the police initially failed to recover any of the missing equipment prompting Carrack to take the drastic step of making an appeal on the December edition of BBC1's Crimewatch.

In the process Paul made history by becoming the first musician to perform on the show when he opened the episode with an acoustic version of How Long.

The appearance on Crimewatch would lead to a happy ending three months later when Carrack was finally reunited with his equipment, thanks to some eagle-eyed detectives.

"They went to interview these guys about doing armed robberies," a grateful Carrack thanked, "and out of coincidence they had one of the guitars that had actually been on TV. The police recognised and found the whole lot in a lock up so now we've got two lots of gear."

Despite the upset of losing his equipment Paul could reflect on the fact that the years between 2000 and 2003 marked something of a career peak.

In fact, Carrack would regard his first three albums for his own label as his best: "They're the ones I think hold up and I believe are a fair representation of me and what I'm about. Some solo albums I made were influenced by people who with the best intent in the world trying to help me be successful, and I tended to sit back and value these people's opinions more than my own. But now I'm very much the big cheese in my own little world and I enjoy it, it's a bit of an ego trip if you like."

"Overall I think it was a very good move because I feel much more independent and in control of my own small world. I think this has a liberating effect on me artistically, because I am not watching my back half the time expecting the rug to be pulled from underneath me."

Chapter Eleven

Having worked so hard to establish himself as a solo artist it was somewhat surprising that Carrack should choose, at the start of 2004, to return once again to the Mike and the Mechanics fold.

Although Carrack had repeatedly expressed his reluctance to pursue any further Mechanics projects following the death of Paul Young, he had continued to write with Rutherford (with B.A. Robertson also sporadically involved), albeit on a casual basis.

Eventually it became clear that they had enough material for an album and, although one gets the strong sense that it wasn't a decision that was taken lightly, Rutherford and Carrack decided to record what would become the band's sixth studio album, Rewired.

"I always felt uncomfortable continuing without Paul, especially on stage," Carrack confirmed. "I was beginning to establish myself as a solo artist outside Mike and the Mechanics and would have been happy to have got on with that but a group decision was made to continue and I agreed that it would be a shame to let it go."

It should be noted that Rutherford was also highly conscious that something had changed: "It was a terrible shock to lose him as a friend and for his family to lose him. Work wise, it affected us in that we thought it was the end of the band and we weren't going to work together anymore. Then over the last four years this new project emerged but not at a very fast pace, partly because we felt that we didn't just want to carry on like nothing had happened."

To reflect Paul Young's absence and the equality of Paul Carrack's own role within the group's framework (he co-wrote all nine songs on the album), Rewired (co-produced by Rutherford and the returning Peter Van Hooke) would be credited to Mike and The Mechanics and Paul Carrack.

"We wanted to emphasize it more, by explicitly listing his name," Rutherford elaborated. "Many do not know who Mike & The Mechanics truly are. And some do not know that Paul sings. It will also show that this is now a slightly different project [and] Paul Young is no longer there."

The album was intended to mark a departure from the sound on M6 and a return to the earlier, more experimental Mechanics sonic template, as Paul explained: "I think the idea with Rewired was to be ambitious musically. I think we felt that the Mike and the Mechanics sound had become a bit safe. The first Mike and the Mechanics album was, at the time, fairly progressive, sonically and it was felt that we should attempt to utilise the many technological innovations and embrace Mike's 'progressive' background to get back to being a bit more 'cutting edge' for want of a better word. Not sure we succeeded but we tried."

If their intention was to do something more experimental they certainly succeeded on the album's opening track, One Left Standing. The song starts with simple drum and bass groove and builds throughout the song with the introduction addition of various layers and textures - tape loops, samples, treated sounds, the novel addition of female backing vocals and only the occasional contribution from Rutherford's guitar.

Although it was odd to hear the Mechanics in such a contemporary setting - which certainly polarised opinion among the band's fans - Carrack and Rutherford deserved praise for taking a few risks. It would have been all too easy to make Rewired a Paul Carrack soul infused solo outing or an album full of Over My Shoulder type chuggalongs and, for what it's worth, I think the results are surprisingly effective on this track, which was earmarked as the album's lead off single.

The Genesis-esque If I Were You was a tad more conventional with some nice chord changes and an especially fine Carrack lead vocal. Although there can be little doubt that Carrack would have approached this differently had it been on one of his solo records, he and Rutherford get the balance between sonic experimentation and their band's more recognisable style right on this track delivering one of the stronger numbers on the album.

Although Perfect Child also keeps the sonic adventurousness to a low-mixed minimum, the lyrics dealing with a parent's aspirations for their children are a bit syruppy for my tastes. Carrack, though, as a father of four, puts the song across well with sincerity and emotion.

After the album's most straightforward song, the oddball title track comes as a bit of a jolt, so much so that its inclusion here seems like a mistake was made at the pressing plant. For a man primarily known for his blue-eyed soul it was strange to find Carrack involved in this industrial, kitchen sink collage of effects, white noise, random stops and starts, overdriven guitar noodles, vocoder-ed vocalisations and Uncle Tom Cobley. Although Carrack and Rutherford did deserve praise for not playing it safe, this, it could be argued, was a step too far.

The strummy singalong I Don't Want It All (with its hint of Over My Shoulder on the chorus) and the epic-sounding How Can I? therefore act as a breath of fresh air after the clanging title track. Both were much more in keeping with the recognisable Mechanics style, and although each has its share of treated sounds and effects Carrack and Rutherford again build a much more satisfactory bridge between the old and newer sounds.

Falling meanwhile starts off with a stabbing synth brass figure that wouldn't have sounded out of place on a James Bond soundtrack before giving way to a spartan descending verse where Carrack's voice is supported by the sort of guitar sounds that Massive Attack had patented. The song then devolves into a massive chorus which, while catchy and more in keeping with earlier Mechanics' work didn't necessarily fit the mood of rest of this song.

One of the album's highlights, though, was the last vocal cut on the album, Somewhere Along The Line, an impressive easy swinging ballad on which Carrack and Rutherford gel wonderfully well, the former offering a wondrous and sensitive vocal, the latter adding a beautifully tasteful acoustic guitar solo. It does seem odd that when you have one of the best blue eyed soul singers in the business and easily one of the world's richest guitar players that they even considered putting instrumental sound collages on this album and it is to that that they return on the album's final piece, Underscore.

More linear and satisfying than the title track, Underscore builds up from its low-key ambient intro to become an infectious guitar-dominated groove before ending abruptly. Although Underscore might have worked better as the soundtrack to an advert for a Prius car, I have to admit I rather like it, despite the fact that its sequencing at the end of the album ends the record on a rather anti-climactic note.

Even though the album's release in July 2004 came with the innovative sop of a DVD that included specially commissioned animated videos to accompany each song, the album could only reach #61 on its initial release (later, when it was reissued, bundled together with the Hits compilation in place of the DVD, the album climbed to #42).

Although this was a disappointment compared with their previous albums, in actual fact the album did well to even chart. The five-year gap since M6, the death of a key member, the radical departure from their radio-friendly sound, the inclusion of only nine tracks (two of which were instrumentals) and the lack of a lead single was not the sort of hand of cards that guaranteed success, but what really sealed the album's fate was the almost blanket media indifference that greeted its release and the lack of a full-scale UK tour. One also got the distinct impression that neither Carrack nor Rutherford were particularly pleased with the album.

In fact, Rutherford later called the album "dodgy."

"I look back at it and you know... we made the record, I didn't think too much about it," he admitted, "but later - I probably should not have done it. The chemistry with Carrack and Young was great, then we lost Paul Young and I kind of battled on - with some nice songs. I shouldn't have done it. And the sound on that - I don't like it."

Unfortunately the critics agreed.

"Yet much as before," quibbled Classic Rock Magazine, "the familiar transatlantic earnestness of Carrack's voice runs through this reasonably tuneful but undistinguished set. There's the occasional flutter of electronic rhythms trying desperately to be modern, but this mainly sounds like a hit 80s album that's had its rhythm tracks brushed up at the remastering stage.

If I Were You is a fair approximation of a late 80s Genesis ballad, a glimpse into what a seamless transition it would've been if Banks and Rutherford had coaxed Carrack into the line-up when Collins quit. Falling is also atmospheric in a way that combines Mama-period you-know-who with John Barry-style orchestral stabs. Despite these relative highlights, there's nothing of the caliber of, say, Silent Running. And like most previous Mechanics outings, it doesn't even hint at the heights some of the participants were capable of in their pomp."

Despite the previous decision not to tour without Young, Rutherford and Carrack did do a few dates in Europe to promote Rewired (backed by Gary Wallis on drums, Jamie Moses on guitar, Rupert Cobb on keyboards, Peter Van Hooke on percussion and three female backing singers), including several dates supporting Phil Collins on his First ... Final Farewell Tour during June and July 2004.

The only UK date the band would undertake, however, would be at the Shepherds Bush Empire in Aid of the Nordoff-Robbins Music Therapy charity on 7th September.

Although fans would not have been aware of this at the time the concert would effectively mark the last time Carrack would appear as a Mechanic. It is perhaps fitting, then, that the band should release the concert (their first live souvenir) on DVD the following March.

A little over a fortnight later Carrack and Rutherford did get together for another concert performance but it was clear even by then that the Mechanics were already unofficially over. This time the event was the The Strat Pack concert at Wembley Arena to mark the 50th Anniversary of the Fender Stratocaster guitar and would also feature, among others, Joe Walsh, Gary Moore, Brian May and David Gilmour.

Although Paul and Mike played a brief four-song set, Mechanics tunes were highly conspicuous by their absence. Carrack and Rutherford opted instead to perform All Along The Watchtower, While My Guitar Gently Weeps, How Long and the Genesis hit I Can't Dance (that the Mechanics had occasionally included in their sets with Paul Young on vocals). Regrettably it was a fairly uninspired performance, one that was captured forever by the concert's release on DVD, ending the Mechanics era on something of a whimper.

"To be honest I wasn't very comfortable about continuing as were because basically it was just Mike and myself left," Carrack justified. "But I think Mike convinced me that we had worked hard to establish ourselves and that people enjoyed the music and that we should continue so we did; we got together, we made an album and we did a few shows, we went on tour with Phil Collins and it was fine, it was good, people accepted it. But it obviously was not going to be the same. Paul was a major part of the band and a great performer and a very popular performer so I felt that we should leave it."

Although Carrack wouldn't formally announce that he had quit the Mechanics until 2006, the Live at Shepherd's Bush DVD marked the end of a partnership with Mike Rutherford that had spanned twenty years. Although his work with the band hadn't always been fully representative of Carrack as an artist, it had been an undeniably successful association - spawning seven hit albums, several smash hit singles on both sides of the Atlantic, umpteen sell-out tours and in The Living Years the hall pass to rock and roll immortality.

Rutherford (who would later form another Mike and the Mechanics with Andrew Roachford and Canadian actor/singer Tim Howar), graciously conceded that it was time for Carrack to move on: "It didn't feel quite right, something had changed, the chemistry had gone. I think certain things have times and eras and after that tour I know I was talking to Paul and my manager saying do you want to give it a go and I think Paul felt he'd done his time, he'd served his time, his sentence."

His sentence served, Carrack returned to his solo career and was soon touring again with his band.

As if to mark the fact that he had returned to his solo career, September 2004 would see the release of the Paul Carrack At The Opera House DVD, filmed at Buxton in January which received very good reviews.

"This DVD should be snapped up by the faithful," applauded David Randall in the Independent on Sunday, "because it is a well-filmed and performed souvenir of Carrack's stage act featuring songs from current album, a few standards, and of course his best-known tunes ... You can't help admire, though, Carrack's honesty. He gets out and about in the regions, directs his own record label and career, and family values are the priority. These are attributes with which an ageing audience can identify. If Carrack could also offer financial advice and foreign travel, he'd clean up."

Carrack's profile was given a further boost when, at the end of 2004, he was invited to participate in the prestigious and highly-rated Jools Holland's 12th New Year's Eve Hootenanny (alongside Eric Clapton, Amy Winehouse, Jamie Cullum, Ian Hunter, Basement Jaxx, Natasha Bedingfield, Mavis Staples and Franz Ferdiand).

"Jools and I go back quite a way and over the years I've met him on many occasions and it was great to get the chance to be on the show," Carrack thanked, "it's probably one of the few credible music shows we've got and a lot of people want to get on it so I was delighted to get the chance."

****

Throughout 2005 Carrack continued to tour extensively and although he seemed in no rush to record a new album of original self-penned material there would be no shortage of product from Carrack-UK.

In fact Christmas 2005 would see the release of another DVD - Paul Carrack Live In Liverpool (recorded at the Liverpool Philharmonic in October 2004) - and an album of Christmas classics (as well as versions of Louis Armstrong's What A Wonderful World and Carrack's own Beautiful World) entitled Winter Wonderland.

The Christmas album (the majority of which was remarkably recorded in two days) would see the realisation of a dream for Carrack, granting him as it did the opportunity to work with Germany's world famous SWR Big Band.

"I love the idea of a new challenge," he would say. "I think a lot of my influences as a singer are from soul music and it's only one more step towards jazz and blues and I like to listen to great jazz singers like Ella Fitzgerald and probably one of my all time favourites is Ray Charles, so for me it's not a career move it's more about having fun playing with the big band and doing these great songs."

The album was later repackaged in Germany as A Soulful Christmas (with the addition of Silent Night and Aretha Franklin's I Say a Little Prayer) and proved to be another strong seller.

"The album raised a few sceptical eyebrows in some quarters," Paul remarked, "but I really enjoyed the challenge of singing with a big band and I believe some of the performances are as good as anything I've been involved with."

Although there was still no sign of an album of new self-penned material, the second half of 2006 would prove to be filled with red-letter days for Paul. Firstly, in June, his much beloved and long out-of-print Suburban Voodoo album was finally issued on digitally remastered CD through Arcadia Records. Remarkably this marked the first time the album had been officially available on CD in the UK.

The following month saw the release of Sam Moore's Overnight Sensational album which included a cover of Carrack's Ain't No Love, on which the soul legend duetted with Stevie Winwood (an artist to whom Carrack had often been compared).

And there was further cause for celebration in October when the Eagles included their cover of I Don't Want to Hear Any More (that Carrack had written for his friend Timothy B. Schmit), on their long-awaited and long-gestated Long Road Out of Eden album.

"I've known the Eagles for a long time and Timothy B. Schmit asked me to give him a song for the album because they'd rejected everything he'd written," Carrack disclosed. "I sent them a demo; they played around with it a bit before recording it exactly as I'd written it, which is always nice for a songwriter. I was delighted they included it."

The band's first album of wholly new material for twenty-eight years Long Road Out of Eden would go on to sell 3.5 million copies in the United States alone, while in the UK, the album quickly sold more than 800,000 copies and was the sixth best-selling CD of 2007, on the basis of just nine weeks on sale.

The song was also released as the album's fifth single and reached #23 on the US Adult Contemporary chart.

Since Carrack almost certainly didn't need the massive amount of money this would have generated (a windfall from which he said he spent "a good deal on some new suits") he seemed touchingly more delighted that the album also included his old friend Frankie Miller's Guilty of the Crime.

October 2006 also saw of the release of The Story So Far, a well-chosen nineteen-track anthology spanning the entirety of Carrack's career.

Beautifully packaged with some lovely candid photographs (including one on the cover, taken by his father, of a young Paul proudly sporting his new Sheffield Wednesday kit) and some detailed liner notes, fans were given another incentive to buy the album due to the newly recorded versions of The Living Years, Love Will Keep Us Alive and a breathtaking, as-nature-intended rendition of Dedicated.

Although the latter was how it should have been originally presented (in my view) this arrangement came about purely by chance, as Carrack explained: "One night on a promotional trip to Holland where I was plugging my new album Groove Approved I stopped by Radio Veronica to do an interview with the legendary DJ Big Al Lagarde. During the interview I did an impromptu version of Dedicated at the upright piano which gained the approval of Al and he kindly played that version of the song on his show many times. I've no idea what became of that recording so I recorded a new version. Cheers Al."

On the back of these considerable triumphs Carrack hit the road again, kicking off his latest tour on 8th October at the Cliffs Pavilion, Southend and continuing into 2007 (concluding with a show at Chesterfield's Winding Wheel Theatre on 4th February).

When the tour was over Carrack returned to the studio to record his eleventh solo album, Old, New, Borrowed and Blue.

As the title implies though, this was something of an archive collection, drawing its songs from a eclectic variety of sources - a couple of Nick Lowe songs (What's Shakin' On The Hill? and Raining, Raining), a solo version of Don't Dream It's Over (that Paul had recorded as a duet in 1991 with the other Paul Young), Ride On (a track recorded with Dutch outfit Gare du Nord for their album Sex 'n' Jazz), two Marvin Gaye covers (What's Goin' On and Ain't That Peculiar), a bluesier, almost gospelly version of Battlefield, a new version of Love Will Keep Us Alive (with his occasional backing singer Lyndsay Dracass and an eighteen-piece string section), a couple of remixes (Always Have, Always Will and No Easy Way Out), a faithful cover of The Beatles' Girl (that Carrack had recorded for a Lennon tribute aired the previous year on Radio 2), and The Reason Was You, Paul's version of the much-covered Kris Kristofferson classic which featured Bob Loveday on violin.

Although it's difficult to regard Old, New, Borrowed and Blue as anything more than a stop gap until he could find the time between tours to record an album of brand new self-penned material, Carrack was not capable of making a bad album and there was plenty on the album to enjoy, particularly the trio of Nick Lowe tracks and the pair of Marvin Gaye songs which, although facsimile recreations, suited Carrack down to the ground.

Fortunately Carrack fans didn't have too long to wait before he did have enough new material for the self-deprecatingly titled I Know That Name, released in October 2008.

Once again Carrack played virtually all the instruments again although he now appeared to recognise this was akin to biting off more than he needed to chew: "Every time I get half way through a project like this I say, "I'll never do it again" because it's just so much work. It just seems to evolve that as I start to write the basic songs, I start to develop them by adding instruments and gradually build them up and then it starts to sound how I want it to sound so I have to go the extra mile and complete it."

The album kicks off with its lead single, a dubby cover of the Bobby 'Blue' Bland track - Aint No Love In The Heart Of The City (recorded with help from producer Peter Collins).

"I always liked the Bobby Bland song and we have been playing it at soundchecks so I went ahead and recorded it," Carrack essayed. "I was mortified when I heard about Mick Hucknall's tribute to Bobby album [Tribute to Bobby, released in 2008], but relieved (and surprised) he didn't do this song as it's probably one of Bobby Bland's better known. I can only imagine that's why he didn't do it."

Although I Don't Want To Hear Any More had been written for The Eagles it was only natural that Carrack should want to put his own spin on it. Joined by Don Henley and Timothy B. Schmit on backing vocals the results are spectacular, effortlessly surpassing his friends' version.

It Ain't Easy to Love Somebody was another of those great Carrack songs that can warm you up on a cold dark night or simply make you feel good, with its era-perfect brass riffs, diminuendos and crescendos and armour-plated chorus this was Carrack doing what he does best - offering cool, burnished soul with sophistication, passion and honesty.

Up next is the the snaky No Doubt About It which, like the track that precedes is the sort of thing Carrack should have been doing on One Good Reason or Groove Approved when he had major record label backing. Had he done something like this there's a good chance he would never have called this album I Know That Name.

With its superbly arranged backing vocals and horns (from Steve Beighton on sax and Ed Collins on trumpet) and this was Carrack at his most vintage sounding. Sometimes words aren't enough to do justice to Carrack's awesome talent, just seek out this track and listen to it on repeat with the volume turned up.

I Don't Want Your Love (I Need Your Love) meanwhile with its seductive string arrangement and smouldering vocals has a hint of Dionne Warwick's Walk On By about it, while Stay Awake (I'm Coming Home) written with Chris Difford, sounds like the best song Ray Charles never recorded. Both tracks offered further proof that when it came to writing soul music that harked back to earlier eras, Carrack truly had no contemporary equal.

Showing an impressive reluctance to stand still creatively, and a commitment to evolving artistically Carrack would surprisingly include two reggae tunes on I Know That Name: Just 4 Tonight and a reggaefied remake of Eyes of Blue.

"I did two tracks on this album that had more of a kinda reggae feel to it," Carrack explained, "and that's because I met a guy called Michael Martin who produced a couple of things in the past for UB40, I actually wrote [Just 4 Tonite] as a ballad and then changed the lyric here and there and gave it this kind of reggae feel."

Having 'done' Ray Charles, Carrack next turns his attention to Sam and Dave on the rousing Love is Thicker than Water (written with Chris Difford).

"When I was writing this particular song, Love's Thicker than Water for my current album, I always thought in the back of my mind I should ask Sam to sing this, it would be fantastic. So I got in touch with him and asked him if he fancied doing it and he came back immediately and said, "yeah, great." So that's one to tell the grandkids - I'm singing a duet with the great Sam Moore!"

Joy pours out of Love's Thicker than Water and Carrack's and Moore's voices blend so naturally, it made you wish they could have done an entire album together.

Carrack continues the R&B vibe with the smooth If I Didn't Love You and the snare-drum heavy Who Am I? (on which Carrack impresses on electric guitar) before concluding the album with the loungy, Burt Bacharach styled Am I In That Dream? - a touching rumination on getting married, setting up house and bringing children into the world.

The song particularly pleased Carrack's co-writer, Chris Difford. "He sent me the final version of the album before last when he'd written some tunes to my lyrics," Difford complimented, "and I just listened to them and I cried my eyes out because they were exactly how I imagined them to be and he touched the spirit inside me that no other writer really touches and that is a lot to do with the way he voices songs."

When I Know That Name was later given the deluxe treatment it came with two bonus cuts - a cover of The Hollies' He Ain't Heavy, He's My Brother and a stunning version of The Temptations' Soul To Soul recorded with The London Community Gospel Choir. Although Carrack had ventured into gospel territory before (and had worked with the L.C.G.C. before, performing The Living Years on their Live At Abbey Road: 21st Anniversary Concert album in 2003) this was in another league entirely. Soul to Soul was spine-tinglingly good and it was even chosen as the single of the week in the Metro newspaper when it was released in April 2010. To promote the single Carrack and the choir would perform the song live on Terry Wogan's Weekend Show with frankly euphoric results.

The album was another unqualified triumph for Carrack - designed to delight his existing fans and attract new admirers - and it was just great to have a new album proper, effectively after a five-year wait since It Ain't Over. Reviewers seemed equally keen to have him back.

"If vocal talent equalled financial success, Paul Carrack would be a bigger name than legends such as Phil Collins or Elton John," opined Record Collector. "That said, Carrack has built up a large, loyal following over the years, and this album, ... should further bolster his reputation as a first-rate singer, songwriter and keyboardist. I Know That Name plays to Carrack's strengths, largely consisting of mellow, Al Green-ish tracks that provide a sympathetic setting for his soulful voice. This is clear from the opening track, an excellent take on Bobby "Blue" Bland's Ain't No Love In The Heart Of The City, superbly arranged with a modern-meets-classic soul sound setting the tone for what follows. Carrack's original material is strong too, one highlight being the sharp Stay Awake (I'm Coming Home), co-written with Squeeze's Chris Difford. The warm, uncluttered production allows plenty of room for Carrack's vocals to shine and he's never sounded better."

"Even though Carrack's solo albums have been generally solid, none have quite risen to the level of consistent engagement as I Know That Name" praised Chris Rizik of SoulTracks. "There isn't a wasted note on the disc, not one 'filler' cut. It's all meat, and Carrack delivers it with aplomb. For lovers of the kind of soulful pop that Hall & Oates, Michael McDonald and Bobby Caldwell brought back in the day, there is still an artist who is delivering the goods, just as he has for four decades. Ladies and gentlemen, please meet Paul Carrack...again. Highly recommended."

To assist with the promotion of I Know That Name and the running of Carrack-UK, Paul teamed up with Stiff records co-founder Dave Robinson (credited on the album as Executive Producer).

"Dave contacted me recently and felt he could help me, in an advisory capacity, to run my label more effectively," Paul divulged. "Obviously he has a wealth of knowledge in all aspects of the music business and apart from relieving me of much of the day to day co ordination of promotion etc. he has many creative ideas and opinions about music and is a great sounding board. He is a 'glass half full' man where-as I am 'glass half empty' so it seems to work well."

Paul later revealed that it had been Robinson who had secured the services of Henley and Schmit on I Don't Want To Hear Any More: "I've got to admit I would never have dreamt of asking them myself and people have always said that to me over the years, "why don't you get Eric Clapton to play ... why don't you get the Eagles?" ... I would never do that, I didn't even ask the Eagles it was [Dave] and he has a lot more of a thick skin than I do and he was like, "Let's give them a call," and they said, "Yeah, we'll do that.""

For I Know That Name, Carrack-UK stepped up the promotional pace a little, releasing five singles from the album, all of which received a great deal of airplay and made I Know That Name his best seller since Satisfy My Soul.

Another album naturally meant another tour. In fact one gets the impression that album-tour-album-tour was the only life Carrack knew.

"Well, I'm not getting any younger so the touring is physically quite demanding," he would say whilst promoting I Know That Name, "but I'm enjoying it so much that I hope I can continue for a long time to come. As a solo artist the live thing has never worked so well for me and in many ways I feel that I am in my prime. I guess if people stop coming that will be the time to slow down."

Paul was clearly in no mood to slow down. And why should he even consider doing so when there were so many new and exciting challenges left to conquer?

On 15th May 2009, for example, Carrack took centre stage at the LSO St. Lukes in London, headlining Friday Night Is Music Night for Radio 2 and performing a selection of his very greatest hits with his band and the BBC Concert Orchestra.

Later that same month Carrack was similarly honoured to be invited to open for The Eagles on the band's outdoor concerts in Malmo and Aarhus, a role he would also fulfill when his old friends played Glasgow's Hampden Park on 4th July and Arnhem's Gelredome a fortnight later.

After the Glasgow concert Carrack was reunited with Frankie Miller. "It was great to see him at the Eagles concert," Paul would say. "He's not in the best of health but he still has a fantastic spirit and he's a great guy."

More reunions were soon afoot when Carrack contributed vocals to My Baby's Gone on Martin Belmont's The Guest List album and teamed up with Nick Lowe to duet on a plaintive, harmony-rich cover of Merle Haggard's Shelly's Winter Love for American rockabilly legend Bill Kirchen's Word To The Wise album.

"Nick and Paul tell me they had Merle Haggard's Shelly's Winter Love by the Osborne Brothers on a tape while touring the US, and would sing it together on the bus," Kirchen elaborated in the album's liner notes. "Why reinvent the wheel, I thought? I just let 'em at it, and tried to not get in the way."

For fans of Lowe and Carrack, the Kirchen song was manna. The two old friends complementing each other so effortlessly that one wishes they would do an entire album of this sort of thing.

Not that Carrack could ever be accused of making such obvious career decisions, a fact he underlined with his next album.

Chapter Twelve

Displaying his usual, admirable reluctance to stand still artistically Carrack's thirteenth solo album, A Different Hat, recorded with the Royal Philharmonic Orchestra, would see him take a radical departure from his tried and tested formula.

Inspired by his collaboration with the BBC Concert Orchestra and Joni Mitchell's Both Sides Now album (in which the legendary Canadian singer-songwriter reinterpreted some of her own material in an orchestral setting), A Different Hat was a labour of love Carrack admitted he had been itching to make for several years but somehow had never been able to pluck up the courage to proceed.

It was his old friend Peter Van Hooke who finally convinced Paul to take the plunge: "I got together with my good friend Peter Van Hooke and he finally called my bluff on this and said well let's do it and it seemed the right time to do this album."

Van Hooke suggested that they use his friend, long-term Andrew Lloyd - Webber orchestrator David Cullen.

Living as he did in a different musical realm, Cullen was not overly familiar with Carrack's work, but when Van Hooke couriered over some albums the celebrated arranger was immediately smitten: "Peter Van Hooke sent me over some of Paul's CDs and I got to know that warm, rich voice, perfectly in tune and with such natural soul style, and consequently showing no more than the feeblest pretence of reluctance I happily allowed myself to be talked into the project. Meeting Paul for the first time at his home studio I was impressed by his clear understanding of which songs were right for this particular album and very quickly we had the first four or five songs decided and the appropriate keys chosen. Peter had stipulated that the arrangements should be strongly orchestral, inventive with rich harmonies, so I went home to my piano, sharpened a pencil and started doodling."

Two months later the first batch of charts were ready and with the seventy-piece Royal Philharmonic Orchestra (hired at Cullen's suggestion) acting as his backing band, Carrack went into AIR Studios on 28th May to record the first four tracks - I Live on a Battlefield, All the Way, For All We Know and Eyes of Blue.

After booking and paying for the studio Carrack was happy to take a subordinate role once recording began.

"I took a back seat, because I was out of my depth," Carrack admitted. "The orchestra came in, got their dots and did their stuff. We did the whole thing in four three-hour sessions. It sure beats spending weeks in a pokey basement studio fiddling around with a drum machine! It's how they used to make records. Even when I was in Ace – how can I mention Ace in the same breath as the Royal Philharmonic Orchestra?! – our album took two weeks to make, mainly because we were playing football all the time!"

"It was a little intimidating at first but I quickly got used to it. They were very helpful and conscientious. Of course they are the cream of the crop."

For such a large-scale project, the album was made very quickly, as Carrack explained: "We said we'd do four songs on the first session, two of mine and two standards. One was a Nat 'King' Cole song. One was a Frank Sinatra track. We came out of a three-hour session in the studio with four finished tracks. I thought "This is fantastic!""

Since Cullen was committed to orchestrating a musical, A Different Hat was delayed for a couple of months, but as soon as the arranger was available again sessions two and three were booked for July and August - this time in the hallowed Abbey Road studios. Clearly no expense was spared.

"It's my production and I financed it," Carrack conceded. "It's a slight indulgence on my part and it was a challenge musically. But it's an intimate album, it's a mature album and it's a grown up album. I'm trying to interpret some well-known traditional songs but bringing something of myself to them."

A cover of Randy Newman's I Think It's Gonna Rain Today (cut at the suggestion of Van Hooke) got the album off to an exquisite start. Recalling Sinatra's work with Nelson Riddle on, say, In The Wee Small Hours of the Morning or Gordon Jenkins's charts on No One Cares, the orchestral setting seemed utterly tailor-made for Carrack's rich and subtle voice.

It was instantly clear, however, that Carrack had adopted a different vocal approach on this album. "My natural territory is to sing quite loud," he explained, "but it sounds much richer when I bring my voice down. We also found that the lower we made the key, the broader my voice sounded, engendering this intimacy. It's a different technique, it's harder – I couldn't have done this a few years ago. You're learning all the time."

Having set the bar high with the Randy Newman cover, Carrack trumps it with his next selection - Moon River. Although it's difficult to think of a crooner who hasn't tackled Henry Mancini and Johnny Mercer's evergreen, Carrack matches Cullen's gossamer arrangement and breathes new freshness into the song, resisting the temptation to oversing and making the song his own. Paul would later name Moon River as his personal favourite on the album.

The easy-swinging Don't Let The Sun Catch You Crying, meanwhile, was Paul's way of paying tribute to an early musical hero: "With this album we cover a lot of different eras but this is a nod in the direction of the 1960s which was a very influential time for myself inasmuch as it got me very enthused about music, so that's the reason for doing the song."

Although I would have loved to have heard him take a crack at the Ray Charles song of the same name, by choosing a relatively obscure Gerry and the Pacemakers seven-inch, Carrack again shows that this was not going to be simply another 'Insert Name Here ... Sings The American Songbook' (a safer, karaoke route pursued by certain other artists one could name), a fact reiterated by his next selection, Bonnie Raitt's I Can't Make You Love Me.

Carrack had long admired the American singer-songwriter and he does Raitt's best-known song justice here, accompanying Cullen's swooping and heady orchestration with a heartmelting vocal that lures out every atom of the song's emotion.

Next up was a haunting, dramatic version of I Live on A Battlefield which vastly improves upon the bouncy original found on Groove Approved. While the 1989 incarnation was catchy and upbeat this rather disguised the fact that the lyrics were always more romantically disillusioned in tone. Arranging the song at a slower tempo, however, allowed the sadness and regret in the libretto to fully emerge.

Even better was the luscious version of Carrack's own Eyes of Blue. Even on an album that includes such timeless classics as All the Way, Moon River and For All We Know Carrack's own songs not only stand toe to toe with such standards but, it could be easily argued, surpasses them for effectiveness on this record.

Incidentally, Eyes of Blue was one of only two tracks that required overdubbing when Davy Spillane was invited to add some flavoursome Irish pipes (the other being Love Will Keep Us Alive).

After a playful, jazzy take on Peggy Lee's I Don't Know Enough About You (on which Carrack tackles the piano solo and offers some particularly sassy vocal phrasing), a fairly straight reading of Sinatra's All The Way and a charming take of Edith Piaf's If You Love Me, the next Carrack song to get an orchestral make over was Love Will Keep Us Alive.

Although Paul had already recorded two versions of the song on Blue Views and The Story So Far, the version here is the definitive one. Cullen's orchestration is particularly subtle and impressionistic, never threatening to intrude on Carrack's flawless, emotive vocal.

The penultimate track is For All We Know, another of the tracks which virtually every crooner has tackled at some stage or another. It's the Nat 'King' Cole version, though, that Carrack takes as his inspiration here.

"When I'm not working I don't listen to a lot of music," Paul revealed. "And when I do, it's nearly always that soothing music of, say, Nat King Cole. It's music that doesn't want to grab your attention and shake you – when you've brought up four kids you're glad of a bit of peace and quiet!"

This version too might not "shake" the listener but Carrack delivers another languid, crystalline vocal, taking a few risks with the melody line along the way like a veteran jazzer.

Carrack's own It Ain't Over ends the album on a vertiginous high, the cherry on the top of an album that has to rank as one of his best ever.

Special kudos is due to the rhythm section of Don Richardson on double bass and Neil Wilkinson on drums who it seems were given licence to really swing on this track, while Cullen also earns his corn with a busy but ice cool arrangement which Carrack matches with an equally towering and seductive vocal that was an undoubted career highlight.

"It was a challenge, and I'm really pleased we did it," Carrack stated when the album was completed. "To be honest, I don't write songs very often because I'm always looking for something new in the songs I play all the time. Whenever I do How Long I never know where it might lead me. I mean, we're talking the very subtlest of things, such as a change in the phrasing, or how I start a line. That's how I keep playing my old chestnuts – so, interpreting other people's songs is an extension of that."

Carrack was clearly invigorated by the experience of making a record outside his usual comfort zones and hinted, once the album was complete, that it could be the first in a series of songbook records: "I really hope we get to make more records. Maybe next time the hat will be a Stetson or a sombrero. I could go Latino. Who knows? There's a lot of hats to try out!"

When A Different Hat was released the critics were bowled over, coughing up a scrapbook's worth of five-star reviews.

"A Different Hat is that rarity," gushed The Independent, "an album featuring the singer live in the studio with a full orchestra, in the manner once commonplace for an earlier era of crooners. These days, there are precious few singers capable of surviving such naked exposure, but David Cullen's vivid arrangements have been kept in suitable keys, which enables Paul Carrack to inhabit the material comfortably... A commendable success."

To promote A Different Hat Carrack embarked on an extensive forty-four-date tour on which, for the for the first time, he would be joined by his teenage son Jack who played drums for the support act Tinlin and would join his father's band towards the end of the show, playing double drums with Carrack's long-serving sticksman Dean Dukes.

Carrack Junior had been drumming for years and, not surprisingly, it was his Dad who had gotten him started, offering plenty of encouragement as his own father had done with him.

"Yeah, he's been playing in bands for a few years but he needs to go up a notch and see what it's all about," proud dad explained. "My home life is very un-rock and roll. We've got four kids and wanted them to do well at school and go into normal careers where the rewards are directly related to their efforts because we all know how flaky rock and roll can be. It looks like one slipped through the net! I hope he gets something out of it then goes off and finds some kids his own age to play with. On the other hand, he might think, 'This is easy, I don't know what the old man was going on about!'"

"My dad tried me on all sorts of instruments including guitar and keyboards," Jack elaborated. "I guess he was trying to get me to play something I could write songs on, but I got nowhere with them. Then one day, when I was about seven, he sat me on the kit and showed me a beat and that was it – I was away. He left me to it then and I began to get more serious about it when I was fourteen or fifteen."

When Jack joined Tinlin Paul went to see them play he was so impressed that he invited them to act as support on his next tour.

"Jack joining my band kind of evolved," Carrack senior explained, "but having him playing drums with me is great, and he's doing the job purely on merit. I went to see him playing with the group Tinlin. He was playing percussion with them and I liked their songs and thought that they had something as a group, so I invited them on tour as the support band. The initial idea was that Jack would play percussion with them and towards the end of our set, he would join with my band and we would have two drummers, as in the Motown style. We had a knock through with the two drummers and we ended up playing the whole set and everybody in the band loved it. I had a word with Dean Dukes, who has been my drummer for several years, and he was all for Jack coming on board. I wouldn't have taken Jack on without Dean's blessing and it's worked out really well."

In fact it says a great deal about the caliber of the people that Carrack employs that rather than putting Dukes' nose out of joint, his long-serving drummer was nothing but encouraging.

"Dean has been working with my dad for many years now," Jack commended, "so he already knew what kind of things my dad likes and what he would expect to be hearing. That made my job easier because, when I came in, I didn't have to work that out the hard way. Dean gives me tips all of the time. He's very encouraging and playing with him has really helped me."

At the conclusion of the Different Hat tour Carrack would reunite with the Royal Philharmonic (at the end of April 2011) for three intimate and exclusive shows at the Royal College of Music's 400-seat capacity Britten Theatre. Filmed for a DVD release the concerts would see Paul and the Phil perform all the tracks from A Different Hat plus The Living Years and How Long, both given the full orchestral treatment.

Despite being troubled prior to the shows with a virus that had threatened to affect his voice, Carrack positively shone throughout the entire series of concerts, so much so that critics were left with little option but to genuflect profusely: "A heart sweeping three-day tour at the Britten Theatre and Royal Music College in London not only brought back fond memories, but more importantly rounded off one of the most successful music careers of any individual in our time," reviewer Hannah Rampton curtsied. "The combination of Paul and the Philharmonic Orchestra breathed new life into an already classic set list, transforming each song into a modern day hit that is sure to win over new fans. The saxophone solos [played by Snake Davies] in particular [were] inspirational, but the whole orchestra together created the moving atmosphere for one epic night. It was a great night for everyone, the audience enjoyed it so much that by the last song the majority of people were up from their seats and dancing, and the legend himself? Well, he continues to write music history!"

****

Despite his extensive touring commitments Carrack found time to help complete Chronicles, the posthumous solo album by his former Mechanics colleague, Paul Young.

The thirteen-track compilation developed out of some thirty songs that were found recorded in various states of completion after Young's death. Alistair Gordon and Martin Kronlund produced the album with input from Young's Sad Cafe colleagues, and, working together in the studio again for the first time since 2004, Mike Rutherford and Paul Carrack. Carrack not only helped to complete the unfinished songs but also added his vocals to Grace of God, which would prove a wonderful reminder of the vocal chemistry the two men shared, a chemistry that had been sadly underused on the Mechanics' records.

After guesting on Nick Lowe's stupendously good The Old Magic album, Carrack returned to his home studio to record the three-track EP Time to Move On to coincide with yet another tour at the end of 2011 and the start of 2012 (during which he also found time to squeeze in several dates in Germany with the SWR Big Band).

The Time to Move on EP (which contained Time to Move On, When My Little Girl is Smiling and Long Ago) though would merely be an hors d'oeuvre for his fourteenth and most recent studio album, Good Feeling, which Carrack completed at the end of his 2011-12 tour.

"After we did the tour ... I more or less just ploughed straight into getting this album done," Paul stated. "I'd made a start on it before that, but it feels good having it all done and dusted and under my belt. Doing something completely different like the orchestral album helped. That was very mellow and downbeat, so coming back to my normal way of doing things, I wanted it to be upbeat, and it felt that, and very fresh."

Once again Carrack would tackle the majority of the instrumental duties on his own.

"I swear I'll never do it again each time," he laughed. "But gradually, because I play a bit of everything, I start building up the tracks and the next thing I know, I'm doing the bloody lot!"

This time though he would have some company in the shape of Rupert Cobb who assisted with the production and his son Jack who handled the drum duties.

"Recording Good Feeling came about as dad was in the studio trying to put a drum track together for the title track," Jack elucidated. "He was struggling trying to programme this shuffle beat and he wasn't really getting there so I offered to pop in and have a little knock. There's a kit already set up in the studio so I sat down and played through it a couple of times and kind of solved his problem for him! From there, I ended up playing on the rest of the album."

"The main thing I need from a drummer is feel," Carrack asserted. "That's all. I'm not interested in chops. We play songs so I just want a drummer to play the songs with feel and taste, and I think Jack has a good sensitivity for playing songs. He listens and he plays the song and he played on pretty much all of my latest album, Good Feeling, and he did a damn good job."

The appropriately named title track gets the album off to a vibrant and joyously loose beginning. Recalling Love is Thicker than Water on I Know That Name, Good Feelin' About It was worthy of inclusion on any Sam and Dave album - while some fluent Stevie Wonder-esque harmonica blowing gives it an added Motown flavour.

As far as Carrack was concerned the new album had a zest about it, thanks to the stylistic detour he taken on his previous album.

"A Different Hat went off the beaten track a little bit," Paul stated, "but Good Feeling is back to my bread and butter, my normal way of working and I think coming back to it now it has a freshness about it and it is because I took that hiatus.

"I never set out with a theme or a plan it just comes out as it is going to come out. As I say, coming back with this freshness and songs that work with my normal band in a live situation, I also had not a bad year, a lot of good things happened in my life. We had a grandson, my football team got promoted, my daughter graduated from college, there were some good things going on. For me it is a fairly upbeat record, I never sit down and plan any kind of concept or anything, it just comes out how it comes out."

Marmalade Moon (co-written with Chris Difford) and the funky Nothing Without You continues the upbeat mood while I Can Hear Ray was written partly as a tribute to Ray Charles and partly out of nostalgia for his Sheffield childhood when he would hear his brother playing the Genius's records.

"Always loved Ray since my elder brother brought home Ingredients In A Recipe For Soul," Carrack detailed. "But the song is about a guy coming home from the road hearing Ray coming down the stairwell and knowing he's almost home."

After a quartet of upbeat tracks Long Ago (written with Chris Antbaldt) is a more wistful, melancholy affair. On it Carrack poignantly reflects upon his childhood and the city he ultimately left behind, and creates in the process one of his best ever lighters aloft songs.

The autumnal Make it Right meanwhile marks the start of a sequence of three cover versions on the album. "That was written by the Tinlin brothers, Alex and Rolf, who supported us on the last tour and they'll be doing this next one as well," Paul said. "My son did a bit of percussion with them on a showcase, and I popped round and thought they had something, they've got some really great songs."

Next up was Bruce Springsteen's If I Should Fall Behind, a song that Carrack had first performed on BBC Radio 2's anniversary special about the sinking of the Titanic aired the previous April.

"I'm not that familiar with the Bruce Springsteen canon," Carrack would claim, "a lot of it is rock'n'roll, but I was asked to contribute a version of that song to the radio show and so I recorded it with an eight-piece string section, and it's probably gathering dust somewhere today. But I've now done my own version at home for the album."

Continuing the run of cover versions, Paul next essays a more mature and world weary version of Nick Lowe's From Now On, that he had first recorded for Suburban Voodoo.

"From Now On is a lovely song and I don't think I really did it justice a while ago when I was, shall I say, fuelled," Paul considered. "I've experienced things since then so it's the right time to do the song again. It's slower now; we've brought the tempo down."

"I much prefer this version," he added. "It does contain my favourite line by Nick, 'Gonna do my level best to keep my nose clean.'"

The song's simplicity is its virtue and the increased intensity on the outro is deliriously good.

Finally moving away from the covers Carrack next offers two of his best ever self-penned soul tunes - I Don't Wanna Lose Your Love and Time to Move On.

Both find Carrack succeeding in capturing the essence of the soul music he loved as a teenager. Asked how he achieved such authentic sounds, Carrack's response was typically modest: "A lot of it's in the mix," he deprecated. "Things hang together somehow in a certain balance, it's not very scientific, it's all done on feel. The lad who's been helping me with this last album, Rupert Cobb, seems to have a handle on what I'm trying to do, he keeps it earthy. I'm glad that comes over."

With its sunny Fender Rhodes palette I Don't Wanna Lose You wouldn't have sounded out of place on the Philly International label while Time to Move on was a Four Tops chart-topper in all but name. The latter in particular shows that even though he was now in his sixties Carrack could still write great soul music with a bang up-to-date sound. Personally the strength of Carrack's seven songwriting contributions to the album makes one regret that he included five cover versions on the album.

And it is the other two cover versions that conclude the album, Goffin and King's When My Little Girl is Smiling and Thad Jones' A Child Is Born.

When My Little Girl Is Smiling was a song Carrack had loved ever since he had heard it performed by Jimmy Justice when the Liverpudlian singer opened for The Beatles in the early 1960s. Although a big hit for the Drifters, Carrack takes Justice's version as a starting point and essays a more Mersey Beat take, adding the riff from The Searchers Needles and Pins for good measure.

A Child is Born, meanwhile, signs the album off on a tender and personal note. Adopting the lower register he'd used on A Different Hat, A Child is Born once again highlights Carrack's underrated jazz chops while the addition of the Moog synthesiser makes it sound like another song that would have fit snugly onto one of Stevie Wonder's 1970s albums. The song was a beautiful way to round off another superb long player and the little chap who inspired the recording was suitably impressed.

"I became a grandfather earlier this year and A Child is Born is for my little grandson [Jonas]," Carrack told www.walesonline.co.uk. "Actually, his parents played the song to him a couple of nights ago and he approved."

"None of my kids are singers, but Jonas is going to be," Carrack predicted. "We put Classic FM on the radio and he sings along to it already."

If Carrack had once again proved himself incapable of making a bad record, the UK's media proved equally unwilling to qualify their praise.

"... as Good Feeling demonstrates," wrote David Quantick on www.bbc.co.uk upon the the album's release in September 2012, "while Carrack is an adaptable singer and player – he shows very little interest in adapting to today's pop world. A chart tart Carrack is not. Good Feeling is the kind of record that fans of Carrack contemporary Nick Lowe would enjoy – both share an approach that's medium-paced, slow-burning and full of genial intensity, like a slightly more approachable Arthur Alexander.

"This is a record so out of time it's hard to say what era it would fit in, leaving the listener to just go with things, hearing songs that occupy the space they're in now. Well-made, good-natured, tuneful and easy to imagine being performed in a nice warm venue with good bathroom facilities, Good Feeling is aptly-named and most enjoyable."

Not only did the album receive great reviews, and loads of airplay on BBC2 but Good Feeling also became the highest chart placing on the UK album charts of his career to date when it peaked at #46.

To tie in with the release of Good Feeling Carrack received another significant garland when BBC4 aired the documentary, Paul Carrack: The Man With the Golden Voice.

"It was made by a fellow called John Mills," Paul said. "That's what he does. He makes various music-type documentaries and he fancied doing something on me. He came on the road with us, filming me performing with the Royal Philharmonic Orchestra, and came up to film the Sheffield fleshpots and my family. Basically the documentary was about me growing up in Sheffield with my brother John and my mother, rather than just about the stuff I've been up to over the past forty years."

Although it would feature suitably warm tributes and contributions from Carrack's friends and collaborators such as Nick Lowe, Neil Hubbard, Elvis Costello, Chris Difford, Glenn Tilbrook and Timothy B. Schmit, Carrack, humble as ever, had been reluctant to call his celebrity mates: "They wanted me to ask Ringo Starr to contribute as I toured with him but I'm just not like that."

Carrack would even confess that he'd had difficulty watching the show when it was screened on 12th October 2012: "I had to watch it in the dark with a roomful of others, and I hate watching myself at the best of times."

"I was a bit concerned that people might find it a bit boring because there was no scandal," Paul quipped, "just folk saying how great I am."

Shortly after the documentary was aired Paul announced that once his Good Feeling Tour was over he would be linking up with Eric Clapton: "As soon as this tour finishes next March, I'll be joining the Eric Clapton band for a while. I've played on several of his albums and played some gigs with him, mainly for charity, and the invitation to play with him again came last month. Some of the dates will be in the States and there'll be five nights at the Royal Albert Hall."

A new album and tour, a BBC4 documentary, the imminent Christmas release of Paul Carrack: Collected (a three-CD, fifty-track career-spanning anthology) and a phone call from the man they used to call God! No wonder Carrack was a feeling good.

To crown it all, on 17th October he received overdue recognition from the music industry when he was awarded a prestigious Gold Badge from The British Academy of Songwriters, Composers and Authors (BASCA) at a ceremony at The Savoy in London.

"Apparently I get a free lunch," Carrack joked ahead of the shindig. "I said, 'Are you joking? I'm in!'"

Then in its 39th year the Gold Badge Awards are an annual celebration of the achievements of an individuals from all areas of the music industry who have made a special contribution in support of songwriters and composers.

Each year up to twelve recipients are recognised for their work and to illustrate the prestige of the award, among those honoured alongside Carrack in 2012 were Pink Floyd's Nick Mason, Beatles producer Sir George Martin and classical guitarist John Williams.

****

With the Good Feeling Tour approaching its conclusion, on 11th February 2013, Paul was invited to participate in BBC Radio 2's 12 Hours To Please Me show - a day-long celebration marking the fiftieth anniversary of the release of The Beatles' debut LP Please, Please Me.

Lining up at Abbey Road Studios to recreate the landmark album alongside an eclectic mix of guests that included Graham Coxon, Stereophonics, Beverley Knight, Mick Hucknall and old muckers Chris Difford and Glenn Tilbrook, Carrack would perform a masterful version of Misery accompanied by a string section.

When the Good Feeling Tour finally came to an end a few weeks later at the start of March Carrack duly reported for duty with the Eric Clapton band alongside Slowhand's long-time touring partners Doyle Bramhall II (guitar), Steve Jordan (drums), Chris Stainton (piano and keyboards), Willie Weeks (bass), fellow newcomer Greg Leisz (pedal steel guitar) plus Michelle John and Sharon White on backing vocals.

The tour with Clapton would be a special one for the legendary guitarist, marking and indeed celebrating his fiftieth year as a professional musician.

Kicking off on 14th March 2013 in Phoenix, Texas the tour would travel the length and breadth of North America before bringing the show to the British Isles in May for a run of dates which included seven sell out nights at The Royal Albert Hall. After hitting continental Europe the tour would finally wrap on 19th June with a show at the Prague O2 Arena.

During the US leg of the tour, Clapton generously allowed Carrack three solo spotlights - How Long, Tempted and a raucous show-closing cover of Joe Cocker's High Time We Went, and this continued when the tour came to Europe with a cover of Come Rain Or Come Shine and It Ain't Easy replacing the former two.

It says much for the enduring quality of Tempted and How Long that they should remain so popular in the States and a mark of the esteem in which Carrack is held by his peers that Clapton should stand aside for three numbers in his own anniversary show.

After a career of almost non-stop recording and touring you could forgive Paul for at least entertaining thoughts of a comfortable retirement. Not a chance, it seems.

At the time of writing Carrack is busy recording another album and has just announced yet another mammoth tour. Kicking off in mid-October, his latest jaunt will comprise forty-nine dates in the UK alone, keeping him busy until April 2014 (with international dates in February and March yet to be confirmed).

After that, who knows where his muse will take him. Even though he is now into his fifth decade as a recording artist it's clear Carrack has lost none of his determination to keep evolving as a musician.

It's this reluctance to stand still artistically that in so many ways defines him; in fact the musical career of Paul Carrack is almost a potted history of the music of the twentieth century itself.

Although it is soul and R&B music with which Carrack is most commonly associated, his recording and touring career has encompassed prog rock, pub rock, art rock (with Roxy), new wave (with Squeeze), huge-selling slick eighties pop (Mike and The Mechanics), classic rock with Spin 1ne 2we and also included a short stint in ska band Madness and an appearance on indie icons The Smiths' first album, which is before we even mention the diversity of styles he embraced alongside Nick Lowe and on his own solo albums.

As well as leaving his mark in virtually every musical development of the twentieth century, if anything the twenty-first century has been even better for Carrack. Forming his own record label has proved to be an inspired decision - allowing his true identity, after so many years as an habitual team player, to finally emerge.

It's obvious that the decision has had a liberating effect artistically, allowing Carrack to follow his creative impulses free from major record label pressure. The results, whether they have been with gospel choirs, big bands or orchestras or produced and performed entirely on his own have been the best of his career without a shadow of a doubt. Carrack is one of those rare artists who has gotten better with age.

While it may well be that Carrack never did get the deserved lucky break that pushed him into that stadium-filling, Lear-Jet-owning elite, people do know his name, do know his songs and do know and marvel at that unmistakeable voice.

Carrack comes across as too effacing to ever blow his own trumpet but no-one would remotely begrudge him if he did crow about achieving the sort of success and stickability that most musicians can only dream about.

Whereas most artists are lucky to find one hit record that guarantees them ever-lasting fame, with How Long, Tempted and The Living Years Carrack has achieved this at least three times, in addition to countless other hit records in the UK, across mainland Europe (where he remains immensely popular) and in the US.

He's also written songs for and played alongside some of the biggest names in the history of popular music; names like Diana Ross, The Eagles, Tom Jones, Roger Waters, B.B. King, Ringo Starr, Eric Clapton and Elton John, to name just a small sample of those who've sought his blue chip services, simply don't come any bigger.

It is clear that he is and always has been held in the highest of regard by his peers and his loyal fans and the sheer longevity of his career is testament to his vast and undiminished talent.

"I've been very lucky," Carrack, with that characteristic modesty, once said, "with a lot of hard work and determination as well, mind – but I've made music my living. I had the support of my family, which is key. You know, I had to make sacrifices when the kids were young, but then they had to sacrifice things for me as well. All those times I headed off on tour there was no complaining from the wife or kids – they just accepted that was what I had to do."

"I feel," Carrack has said, "that as long as there are people out there interested in what I'm doing and as long as I am producing decent work, I will have the opportunity to keep doing what I love, making music."

Whilst researching this book I've often wished I could have a dubloon for every time I've heard or read Carrack described as "pop music's ultimate journeyman." One can only hope that that journey will continue for a long time to come.

PAUL CARRACK
SELECTED DISCOGRAPHY

PAUL CARRACK

1980   Nightbird

1982   Suburban Voodoo

1987   One Good Reason

1989   Groove Approved

1996   Blue Views

1997   Beautiful World

2000   Satisfy My Soul

2001   Groovin' (repackaged in 2002 as Still Groovin')

2003   It Ain't Over

2005   Winter Wonderland (also released in repackaged form in Germany as A Soulful Christmas)

2007   Old, New, Borrowed and Blue

2008   I Know That Name

2010   A Different Hat

2012   Good Feeling

WARM DUST

1970   And it Came to Pass

1971   Peace for our Time

1972   Warm Dust

1972   Dreams of Impossibilities (German-only highlights compilation of the of their first two albums)

Non-Album Single

1971   It's A Beautiful Day/Worm Dance

ACE

1974   Five-A-Side

1975   Time for Another

1977   No Strings

FRANKIE MILLER

1978   Double Trouble

1979   Falling In Love (issued in the US as A Perfect Fit)

ROXY MUSIC

1979   Manifesto

1980   Flesh and Blood (Carrack appears on Oh Yeah and Running Wild)

1982   Avalon (Carrack appears on To Turn You On)

SQUEEZE

1981   East Side Story

1993   Some Fantastic Place

2010   Spot the Difference (Carrack sings lead on a new version of Tempted)

CARLENE CARTER

1981   Blue Nun

NICK LOWE

1982   Nick the Knife

1983   The Abominable Showman

1984   Nick Lowe and His Cowboy Outfit

1985   The Rose of England

1988   Pinker and Prouder than Previous

1990   Party of One

2011   The Old Magic

JOHN HIATT

1985   Riding with the King

MIKE AND THE MECHANICS

1985   Mike + The Mechanics

1988   Living Years

1991   Word of Mouth

1995   Beggar on a Beach of Gold

1999   Mike & The Mechanics (more commonly known as M6)

2004   Rewired

ROGER WATERS

1985   When the Wind Blows (keyboards and vocals on Folded Flags)

1987   Radio K.A.O.S. (Carrack sings lead vocals on The Powers That Be)

1991   Live in Berlin (Carrack sings lead vocals on Hey, You)

BETH NIELSEN CHAPMAN

1993   You Hold The Key (Carrack duets on In The Time it Takes)

SPIN 1NE 2WO

1993   Spin 1ne 2wo

STEVE HACKETT

1996   Genesis Revisited (Carrack sings lead vocals on Deja Vu and Your Own Special Way)

B.B. KING

1997   Deuces Wild (Carrack contributes organ and sings lead vocals on Bring It Home to Me and Cryin' Won't Help You Babe)

ERIC CLAPTON

1998   Pilgrim (Carrack plays organ)

2001   Reptile (Carrack plays keyboards, wurlitzer and Hammond organ)

2010   Clapton (Carrack plays Hammond organ)

BILL WYMAN'S RHYTHM KINGS

1999   Anyway The Wind Blows (Carrack sings lead vocals on Too Late)

JOOLS HOLLAND AND HIS RHYTHM AND BLUES ORCHESTRA

2001   Small World Big Band (Carrack sings lead vocals on It's So Blue)

RINGO STARR

2003   Tour 2003 (Carrack plays keyboards and sings lead vocals on How Long and The Living Years)

MARTIN BELMONT

2009   The Guest List (Carrack sings lead vocals on My Baby's Gone)

BILL KIRCHEN

2009   Word To The Wise (Carrack duets with Nick Lowe on Shelly's Winter Love)

PAUL YOUNG

2011   Chronicles (Carrack duets with Young on Grace of God)

Carrack's keyboard/organ/piano/ vocals can also be heard on:

1975	Nutz: Nutz Too
1977	Inga Rumpf: My Life is a Boogie
1983	The Smiths: The Smiths
1983	The Undertones: Positive Touch
1983	The Pretenders: Learning to Crawl (Carrack plays keyboards on Thin Line Between Love And Hate)
1984	Robert Ellis Orrall: Contain Yourself
1986	Marti Jones: Match Game
1987	Wax: American English
1990	Bob Geldof: Vegetarians of Love
1990	Aztec Camera: Stray
1995	Elton John: Made in England
1997	Elton John: The Big Picture (Carrack plays organ on Something About the Way You Look Tonight)
1998	Simply Red: Blue
1998	Royal Philharmonic Orchestra: Philharmania (Carrack sings lead vocals on No Face, No Name, No Number)
2003	London Community Gospel Choir: Live At Abbey Road: 21st Anniversary Concert (Carrack sings lead vocals on The Living Years)
2007	Gare Du Nord: Sex 'n' Jazz (Carrack sings lead vocals on Ride On)
2009	Various Artists: We Will Remember Them

Notable other non-album releases

1984	We Love You Wednesday
1989	Romance (duet with Terri Nunn - included on the soundtrack to the film Sing)
1991	Don't Dream It's Over (duet with Paul Young)
1991	It's A Praise For Sheffield Wednesday (credited to Big Ron's Barmy Army)
2000	If You Believe In Me (from the movie Beautiful Joe)
2011	Love Will Keep Us Alive (duet with Timothy B. Schmit)
2011	Thinking about you (This Christmas) b/w This Christmas (Hang up the mistletoe)

Compilation Albums

1987	Ace Mechanic
1988	The Carrack Collection
1994	21 Good Reasons
1995	Carrackter Reference
2006	The Story So Far
2012	Paul Carrack: Collected

DVDs

2001	Paul Carrack: In Concert
2004	Paul Carrack: Live at the Opera House
2005	Paul Carrack: Live in Liverpool
2005	Mike + The Mechanics + Paul Carrack: Live At Shepherds Bush
2007	Paul Carrack: Live At Rockpalast
2009	Paul Carrack: I Know That Name
2010	Paul Carrack: Live in 3D
2011	Paul Carrack: A Different Hat Live at The Royal College Of Music

Warm Dust - Paul Carrack, standing centre
Photograph courtesy of John Surguy